TABLE OF CONTENTS

CONCLUSION
REFERENCES

Constitutional and Legal Issues of Urban Planning and Land Use Control: An Urban Geography Analysis

- **The Issue of Zoning and "Taking"**
- **Zoning and the Land Question**
- **Housing Programs and the Central City**
- **Conclusion**
- **References**

THE AFRICENTRIC SOCIOURBAN PLANNING PARADIGM: DEFINING DEVELOPMENT IN YOUR OWN IMAGE AND INTERESTS

- **Know Your Enemy**
- **Internal Opposition: Provocateurs and Race Traitors**
- **External Opposition: Read and Study the Words of Elites**
- **CASE STUDY - The Geo-Politics of Community Growth: Mayor Mike Fahey's January 2004, "State of the City Address"**
- **Three Approaches to Neighborhood Development: Analysis**

    ✓ The Neighborhood Maintenance Approach
    ✓ The Social Work Approach
    ✓ The Political Activist Approach

AFRICENTRIC SOCIOURBAN PLANNING = RE-EDUCATION
ESSAYS AND EXPOSURE: TWO ARTICLES FROM 1982
CONCLUSION
REFERENCES

Preface

In 1985 the Glenn Frey cut, "You Belong to the City" went a long way toward capsulizing the urban mood that people who live in the city feel and experience. The following lyrics to the song bear that out:

The sun goes down
The night rolls in
You can feel it starting
All over again

The moon comes up
And the music calls
You're getting tired of
Staring at the same four walls

You're out of your room
And down on the street
Moving through the crowd
In the midnight heat

The traffic roars
And the sirens scream
You look at the faces
It's just like a dream

Nobody knows where you're going
Nobody cares where you've been

'Cause you belong to the city
You belong to the night
Living in a river of darkness
Beneath the neon light

You were born in the city
Concrete under your feet
It's in your moves
It's in your blood
You're a man of the street

When you said goodbye
You were on the run
Trying to get away
From the things you've done

Now you're back again
And you're feeling strange
So much has happened
But nothing has changed

You still don't know where you're going
You're still just a face in the crowd

You belong to the city
You belong to the night
Living in a river of darkness
Beneath the neon light

You were born in the city
Concrete under your feet
It's in your blood
It's in your moves
You're a man of the street

You can feel it
You can taste it
You can see it
You can face it

You can hear it hey
You're getting near it hey
You wanna make it whoa
'Cause you can take it whoa

You belong to the city
You belong to the night
You belong to the city
You belong to the night

The city. Most people want to talk about, many lie about being a part of or living in it, but very few understand it.

I attended several graduate schools with courses where, on the first day, we were to introduce ourselves and give some brief background. White folks would claim to be from Chicago, Detroit or Kansas City, but as soon as I heard those claims I lit into them, having lived in Chicago for 2 years myself. My first question would be, "what part of Chicago did you live in"? The white people would hesitate, realizing that they were more than likely speaking to an urban dweller and would shakily claim Bellville or Schaumburg or Cicero. They never LIVED in Chicago. They *fantasized* about living there.

This book, Introduction to Africentric Sociourban Planning, is a modest contribution to what I hope will be a new field of study for community organizers, urban planners and social workers. I operationally define "sociourban" as, "analysis of relationships between urban residents and others and the product of those relations as they relate to the development of and financial risk involved with community growth." This is my concept, my definition and therefore I will accept no black or white opposition to it.

I was blessed enough to go through a Master's program in Urban Studies at the University of Nebraska Omaha and have, as my mentor and friend, a man named Dr. Peter Suzuki. He knew talent when he saw it and after dominating a few classes, he began designing "independent studies" assignments for me so that I would be able to learn more than just generic "urban studies," but would become engaged in the more technical (and to me, more relevant) discipline of urban planning.

I learned a great deal about the local, regional and international aspects of urban planning. After leaving for a doctoral program in sociology, I then applied for and received, a fellowship from the Department of Housing and Urban Development (HUD) through the University of Iowa's Urban Community and Regional Planning program, one of the best in the nation. On a full ride, I stayed there for a year but again, learned so much through reading and study, that I became enamored with the field.

I continue to build a library of journal articles and, upon returning to Nebraska, writing term papers for students in the public administration and urban studies departments. In addition to being lucrative, it was just one more way to digest enormous amounts of information, including several theses and capstone papers along the way.

My pedigree continues to grow. I went on to found the largest African-American neighborhood organization in Nebraska, and in fact, won the "Project of the Century Award" in the year 2000 for the work put in by that group, the Triple One Neighborhood Association and Parents Union. I have filed several grievances against the City of Omaha's planning department and had two consecutive injunctions approved because of that city's abuse of Community Development Block Grant money.

As an urbanologist, I am the founding director of the largest black think tank in the state of Nebraska, the Uhuru Sasa Research Institute and the director of the oldest black neighborhood association, the Triple One Neighborhood Association. I am the editor and publisher of the longest- running black newsletter in the history of the state of Nebraska, the TONA News, a monthly running continuously since June of 2015

In the movie "Birth of a Dragon," the Shaolin master Wong Jack Man taught, "Technique is a trap, style is a prison – unless he is willing to be reborn." This is what American education has become: both a trap and a prison. It's ethnocentric form and function perpetuates the mis-understanding that permeates the world. That is why newer forms and approaches to reality are needed – hence the Africentric Sociourban Planning approach and paradigm.

Put another way, the places where we, as black people, live and operate our lives are both major environmental and sociourban determinants or our present and future growth and development status. One way to address this would be to offer more urban-related courses into the Black Studies curricula of various institutions. Those developing the curriculum might wish to focus on the locality in which the school is situated and in that way make a valuable contribution to local museums and archives.

Another way would be to offer courses in "Black Urban Reality" or some other title whereby those who are non-black and those blacks raised in suburbia could not only learn about the problems and prospects of the inner city, but also about the people who inherited those problems and prospects and how these impact upon the future generations.

Introduction, Explanation, Definitions, Methodology

This is new territory so bear with me while I work to make the information and definitions as categorically determinate as possible. If there are shortcomings, then like the relay person in the race, I shall pass the baton to others who can and will take this proposed field of study and turn it into the guiding community doctrine that it has the potential to become.

Definitions

The Oxford Universal Dictionary defines definition as "A precise statement of the essential nature of a thing." (There are four other definitions related to the root "define" that do not apply here). Webster elaborates somewhat: a definition is "a word or phrase expressing the essential nature of a person or thing or class of persons or things, a statement of the meaning of a word or word group."

Borrowing from Davidson & Dolnick (2004), I will use their three (3) purposes for "definitions" that have a universal applicability and are most relevant to acquiring a deeper understanding of the Africentric Sociourban Planning that I am proposing herein. According to these authors,

In the context of the land development ordinance, definitions have three purposes: 1. Definitions simplify the text. 2. Definitions establish the precise meaning of a word or phrase that may be subject to differing interpretations. Precision eliminates ambiguity and vagueness. It focuses on the essential elements of a word or phrase and clearly marks off and limits its application or interpretation 3. Definitions transform technical terms into an understandable, usable terminology. Definitions give meaning to sometimes abstract, technical terms for the purpose of controlling and guiding development. (Davidson & Dolnick, 2004)

Let's be more specific in terms of the three purposes of a definition.

Simplifying the text is very important because urban planning is a technical area of analysis and study and should not be played with. Terms like "channelization," "hinterland," "moratorium," "tax incremental financing," "eminent domain," "aerial photography," "mixed use buildings," "density bonus," "volume-to-capacity ratio," "grid system," "parcel map", "viaduct" and so many more. So simplification is important so that the concepts shared can be visualized and understood.

Secondly, definitions give precise meanings of words. You have to know what the words mean so that you can use them – even if you are debating their accuracy. And third, the definition transforms technical terms, like some of the ones I've shared, into understandable terms.

This book is written so that the terms that are deemed technical will be clearly discernible and understandable. More profoundly, they will be seen with an eye and ear open for cross cultural competency. There will be no one-way bias in the way that the terms and the area of "urban planning" are presently permeated with. Socrates said that, "The beginning of wisdom is the definition of terms."

"Socio-urban"

The places where we, as black people, live and operate our lives and are both major environmental and sociourban determinants of our present and future growth and development status.

As those of us who are urbanologists already know, Urban planning is a technical and political process concerned with the development and design of land use in an urban environment, including air, water, and the infrastructure passing into and out of urban areas, such as transportation, communications, and distribution networks. This most functional of definitions hails from the 1998 work of Nigel Taylor in his classic, *Urban Planning Theory Since 1945*. Though rife with racial exclusions and biased findings, the book nevertheless provides a necessary basis and foundation for the Africentric Sociourban Planning perspective I am proposing herein.

One need only attend a single class in urban planning and upon hearing the initial and opening presentation by the instructor, realize how ethnocentric and lily-white the field has been and still remains. Do not forget that it was the urban planner who assisted the politicians, the policymakers and the "citizen's groups" to foster and maintain racial segregation. And from there they teamed up to make such segregation and the isolation of "colored" populations the law of the land. Because of this, the need for what is being proposed here is of paramount importance.

For instance, in any introductory level urban planning course, students thirty for understanding of cities, rural life and the transportation systems that were created to link the two, are told from the get-go that "urban planning deals with physical layout of human settlements" (Taylor, 1998). When the word human is used, what is being described is white reality. "Human settlements" do not include the domiciles that were constructed and in existence in Africa and Asia while the white race was living on the fringes of barbarism in Europe. As is the case in courses in Western Civilization and World History, the white point of view in defining settlements and how they were formed is imposed on the academic world and in doing so, those revised myths become "traditional models" for future research and study.

Physical layout is psycho-social, according to the Africentric Sociourban Planning model (hereafter referred to as ASP). What determines the location of the layout goes behind the weather and the type of soil one settles on. There are reasons why people "settle" in certain places. In my book Exodus, I document more than 20 cities in "the North" that black people migrated to from "the South" after finally being emancipated. And pay close attention: much of what they encountered was developed, designed and perpetuated by various forms of "urban planning" groups. The white ethnics from Europe were immediately placed in slums and kept there, a point painted with laser accuracy in photos in Jacob Riis' 1890 book, H*ow the Other Half Lives: Studies among the Tenements of New York*. This is the work that we were told inspired some of the many reforms that took place in housing for working class people. Again, the word "people" means "white people" because Black people's housing as located close to factories and warehouses, areas high in pollution and toxic gases. These facts are at the base of the REAL urban planning.

In addition, Thomas Lee Philpott's (1991), The Slum and the Ghetto: Immigrants, Blacks, and Reformers in Chicago, 1880-1930 (American Society and Culture) explains the role of "design" in maintaining the slum first, for white ethnics and then later because of "ethnic succession," the colored people came in

(Blacks and Latinos) and rented the housing that whites left behind as they ran to the suburbs.

As you can see, "The physical layout of human settlements" are decided upon not only by the "in-group," but also by the "out-group" when it comes to powerless migrants. These are the types of socio-urban issues that the ASP hopes to cover and link to the more technical aspects of urban planning.

During the early courses in urban planning there is much discussion of the "public welfare," and that is usually linked to "the police power." The immediate legal case is Euclid v. Ambler Realty, the first issue regarding "zoning" and while important, it did not address the pervasive racism and discrimination that black people were facing during this same period. This was a 1926 case and Euclid, Ohio was a suburb of Cleveland. During that time Cleveland was racially segregated and there is no mention of this fact when the case is discussed in these urban studies courses.

Another point is that "urban planning" also goes by names like "city planning," "urban development," "and "town planning." But in each of these you will find a gross neglect of discussions of race. The "human settlements" that are of importance are white ones, and blacks do not come into the picture until after black migration to the north. In fact, the black presence in the north accelerated the work of the urban planners to make sure that low-income people and blacks were separated from the "normal white folks." This is the REAL American history.

My concept of Africentric Sociourban planning is not something brand new or sui generis. It just far more humane and the motivations are rooted in the future, not pacification plans for the present. In urban planning we find various forms of planning that attempted to show a concern for and commitment to the black community such as advocacy planning, neighborhood planning and equity planning. Let me briefly address each of these as we learned them in our urban planning courses.

Advocacy planning is,

> Advocacy planning was formulated in the 1960s by Paul Davidoff. **It is a pluralistic and inclusive planning theory where planners seek to represent the interests of various groups within society.** Davidoff (1965) was an activist lawyer and planner who believed that **advocacy planning was a necessary method for representing the low-income and minority groups who were not always on equal footing with the rich and powerful.** (Wikipedia, 2018 – emphasis added).

Do you see how the "definers" hand down information from one generation to the next? That is why I am sharing it with you so you can get an idea what a person with an advanced intellect such as myself, which includes extensive knowledge on black history, has to go through in the classroom.

Before moving to the next model, let me back up what I just alleged. Note that in the previous paragraph the use of the term "race" is not used; note that the term "discrimination" is not used. In their place are euphemistic technical sounding terms – another reason why my Africentric Sociourban Paradigm is so important. It defined itself. But look at what we find if we leave the planning of black communities in the hands of aliens.

First off the claim that advocacy planning is a theory "where planners seek to represent the interests of various groups within society." That ain't sayin' shit. I'm sure that when the white boy was laying out his segregated and redlined city structure, that was a form of "advocacy planning" – advocating for the Klan! But take note that these planners want to do things FOR the community without consulting the community. That's the old paternalistic racism approach – "don't worry niggers – we know what's best." That's why the first word in my approach defines the scope and content of the paradigm: "Africentric."

Secondly, the claim that, "advocacy planning was a necessary method for representing the low-income and minority groups who were not always on equal footing with the rich and powerful." And how long did it take these "planners" to realize that it was time? How many black families were torn apart, how many families died or got sick from unhealthy living standards? Advocacy planning, in my view is not about putting minorities "on equal footing with the rich and powerful," and to assume such a thing is ludicrous. It was about appearing to care and do something while maintaining the status quo. Public housing, placed in the same segregated conditions as the rest of the ghetto, was about as far as these "advocates" appeared willing to go.

Then there is "neighborhood planning." According to one source,

> The purpose of neighborhood planning is to understand **what individual neighborhoods want to become.** To understand this**, public participation of neighbors is absolutely crucial.** In reality, it is only at this level, where the actual number of parties is small, that true democratic decision making may be possible.(Wikipedia, 2018 – emphasis added)

This is insane. You already KNOW what neighborhoods want to become because you (the planners) are the ones who gave form and function to those neighborhoods! You defined the size, the population density, the quality of housing (if there is any), how many apartments exist, how close the housing is to toxic waste dumps like factories and warehouses or how close to waterways that could flood from time to time. So to feign ignorance is not going to work because the neighborhoods were there all along.

The fact is, all neighborhoods want to look viable. No one wants to live in a slum, a ghetto, or a barrio. So again we have distorted language defining a distorted vision. The reliance on "public participation" is not what it seems: these people tend to pick and choose which segments of the "public" they want input from. Usually it's from those who are easiest to control: those beholden to them because of their jobs, ministers and contractors who can hope for jobs once decisions are made. This is not an act of sincere benevolence; it is an act of manipulation.

Finally we have "equity planning."

> Equity planning is a framework in which urban planners **working within government use their research, analytical, and organizing skills to influence opinion**, mobilize underrepresented constituencies, and advance and perhaps implement policies and programs that **redistribute public and private resources to the poor and working class**. (Metzger, 1996 – emphasis added)

Some ideas are written in terms of realistic application and others are more utopian and "wishful." In my view, Equity planning is an example of the latter.

We all know how this society views the concept of "equity:" Whites on top, blacks on the bottom. Picture an Indian totem pole with faces from the top to the bottom. The face on top is the white man and the one on the bottom is represents people of color. If we follow equity planning, we would have to see this as a good thing because although ranked from top to bottom, all faces share the same pole. But that is not what a hierarchy is about and the white man knows it. His concept of "equity" can be seen in his historical treatment of people of color on this country.

The concept of "socio-urban" is, again, about the attitudes and thought processes that give rise to certain types of interactions. This area places an emphasis on the roles of race and ethnicity in these interactions. The pervasive whiteness of "urban planning" is made clear even in its own generic definitions. Again, Taylor (1998):

> Urban planning guides orderly development in urban, suburban and rural areas. Although predominantly concerned with the planning of settlements and communities, urban planning is also responsible for the planning and development of water use and resources, rural and agricultural land, parks and conserving areas of natural environmental significance. Practitioners of urban planning are concerned with research and analysis, strategic thinking, architecture, urban design, public

consultation, policy recommendations, implementation and management … Enforcement methodologies include governmental zoning, planning permissions, and building codes, as well as private easements and restrictive covenants.

All we need do to find further justification or rationale for the ASP is to take the previous paragraph and analyze based upon the impact that what is described has had and continues to have on race relations in America and, more specifically, on maintaining the black ghettos and brown barrios that continue to exist.

By its own admission it is urban planning that "is responsible for the planning and development of water use and resources." Let's stop there for a minute. There is not an urban planning class that I know of that deals with the racist inclinations behind the construction of the levee system and the fact that black people were "steered" toward living near them. There is an old saying about older blacks, "If the good Lord's willing and the creek don't rise." That means if there's not a flood because most blacks were forced to live near wherever there was a body of water.

Think I'm playing? Look at New Orleans and it's levee system and what happened when they broke. Who was hurt the most? Black people. Even though the Great Flood of 1927 hurt black people, we saw that as a positive sign to get up from under the oppressive force of the white man's "sharecropping system." As National Public Radio explained on a segment of "All Things Considered,"

> **The Great Flood meant great suffering and misery for blacks up and down the Mississippi River**. But many also thought of the flood as a harbinger of hope. "African-Americans viewed the flood as an act of God that liberated them," Brown says. "In the 1920s, the vast majority of that black population made their living by sharecropping. Everybody got by on credit. The flood made it obvious that there was not going to be a crop during that year, so they were not facing one year of barely breaking even or being able to pay off debt, but two full years. (National Public Radio, 2011).

Do you think that a course in urban planning, one that claims to be discussing "water use and resources," would ever mention what I just shared with you? Furthermore,

> Some people turned the whole story on its head and said that the Lord had washed away the debt and liberated the black sharecroppers to move on to other employment. Many of them did. **They left the Delta** and participated in the Great Migration and headed north and went to Chicago or Detroit or some other metropolitan area and sought new employment." (National Public Radio, 2011).

And don't think that getting away from all that water wasn't a major consideration. And many still didn't avoid the water because wherever they moved, where there was a river or a major lake, they were going to be "assigned" to live next to it.

But there are more examples from the previous listing of urban planning components.

The claim that the issues of "rural and agricultural land" is covered. Remember what I wrote earlier about the white definition of "settlements"? This is how they view land: as a static essence that was moot until Europeans came along and gave it message, meaning and magnitude. That's why even to this day they talk about "the founding fathers", "the first Americans" and other names they give to their white ancestors, as if there were no First Nation people already inhabiting the land.

This is the same thinking that goes into discussions of "rural and agricultural land." In urban planning they begin with the white farmer and the pioneer "settler". They talk about all the adversity that had to be overcome and how the rural setting evolved with the coming of transportation systems and when that happened cities were formed and could become bigger because of the transportation. All that and no mention of the southern agricultural economy and those million Africans that picked cotton during the days of antebellum enslavement.

The description claims that urban planning covers, "parks and conserving areas of natural environmental significance." The concept of the formation of the park system is a glaring example of white nationalism, plain and simple. As one source explains it,

> Since 1872 the United States National Park System has grown from a single, public reservation called Yellowstone National Park to embrace over 450 natural, historical, recreational, and cultural areas throughout the United States, its territories, and island possessions. These areas include a diverse varieties of areas —National Parks, National Monuments, National Memorials, National Military Parks, National Historic Sites, National Parkways, National Recreation Areas, National Seashores, National Scenic Riverways, National Scenic Trails, and others (Wikipedia, 2018).

Their words, not mine. Witness their concept of the parks begins in 1872. Where did they get the land? Or yeah: they stole it from the First Nation people and just laid claim to it. So with the land they snatched, they build a national temple of worship to themselves through parks and monuments. These places do nothing short of paying homage to white nationalism. That brings us to the second point, the conserving of the areas of "natural environmental significance."

And that means the areas just cited. They have a special Department at the federal level and they have a major budget. They preserve these places so that the public can come and visit them. And in doing so you are pledging yourself to white history. Urban planners aren't going to tell the truth about the purpose of these parks and monuments. The purpose of traditional urban planning s not to tell THE truth, it is to tell A truth.

The previous description also claims that "practitioners of urban planning "are concerned with research and analysis, strategic thinking, architecture, urban design, public consultation, policy recommendations, implementation and management … (Taylor, 1998).

You can be "concerned with" something and still be biased in the application of those concerns. For instance, white folks were concerned about the agricultural economy of the southern united states and they expressed that concern by going over to Africa, kidnapping African people and forcing them to work that land until the southern economy was number one in the world. See? "Concern" and "compassion" can oftentimes be two different things.

Research and analysis are moot if you conduct either one with a preconceived bias. Strategic thinking, geared toward "empire building" is biased in and of itself. But what about the African empires that would have been built had not architects, engineers and scholars been kidnapped along with others to get on a ship, come to these shores, and be forced into hard labor? Will urban planning cover THAT?

From there the rest is an exercise in white nationalistic nation building. Architecture with buildings named after other white men even when men of color worked on those buildings, urban design meant to mystify and change the skyline as if an homage to the white man as some kind of "god," public consultation which is white men talking with other white men to keep men of color out, policy recommendations and so on. Urban planning is the key to the isolation of people of color from the white mainstream, which has long been their goal. And it is a goal that is maintained even to this day in 2018.

Urban planning also covers the quasi-legal and judicial components of land use and land control. Taylor adds, "Enforcement methodologies include governmental zoning, planning permissions, and building codes, as well as private easements and restrictive covenants." Those private easements and restrictive covenants – which I have written extensively on – were meant to inform white homeowners and others who would venture into a given area that there were "no niggers allowed." Urban planners cannot cover these issues because these issues are an essential part of their ethnocentric duties! Put another way,

> Urban planners work with the cognate fields of architecture, landscape
> architecture, civil engineering, and public administration to achieve
> strategic, policy and sustainability goals. Early urban planners were often
> members of these cognate fields. Today urban planning is a separate,
> independent professional discipline. The discipline is the broader
> category that includes different sub-fields such as land-use
> planning, zoning, economic development, environmental planning,
> and transportation planning (Wikipedia, 2018)

It sounds repetitious but it is more academically acceptable. You need not mention the term "white," "Anglo," or "Caucasian" to know quite readily that this is the group that urban planning quite literally serves. What Douglas Massey and Nancy Denton dubbed "American Apartheid" in 1993 is the product of the racist mentality, quite true. But the hand that stirred the pot, mixed the ingredients, and produced the "meal of malice," the "rudiments of racism," the "stew of segregation" and served the "dinner of discrimination" was none other than the urban planner.

In sum, the Africentric Sociourban Paradigm is an idea whose time has come and rests on a present-day as well as a futuristic tenet – leadership by people of color FOR people of color with the future of a "browning of America" being inevitable. White people can no longer teach what they don't know and lead what they don't know, as has been the traditional tendency and historical pattern.

A Critique of Amanda Erikson's "Brief History of the Birth of Urban Planning": African-American Analysis and Assessment

White nationalism ruled supreme in the United States and, as such, it was inevitable that it would trickle down to the people who were planning the cities, known then as "city planners."

This was not just a national reality: it was international. Take note of the following:

> At America's first urban planning conference, held in New York
> in 1898, *a British planner* asked whether he and his colleagues
> were striving for beautiful people or beautiful cities. Is urban
> planning about physical design, he wondered, or about making
> things easier for the people who live in our urban spaces?
> It was an essential question for the field, which really wasn't born
> until the early 20th century (Erikson, 2012 – emphasis added).

I have been in higher education as a student, counselor and teacher since 1973. I have debated and otherwise interacted with the best minds that the white race has to produce. And no matter what their background or pedigree, I have found one constant: when they come across new information or insights, and if those insights are not in the best interests of their race – no matter how well documented – *they will go into escapist denial mode and retreat from the conversation.* Please refer back to the previous section where the importance of definition was laid out.

At any rate, I have also found this ethnocentric and revisionist tendency in their writings.

The article that I am about to critique is written by someone who has obviously researched "a history" of urban planning. But the mistake that she makes, akin to the one that most white scholars make, is that what they produce is usually presented as THE history, THE story, THE psychology and so on. It is almost as if just because they write it, what they write about becomes validated.

I mention these points because Ms. Erikson has documented many of the most essential facts of the evolution of urban planning, but she omits key factors that revolve around white supremacy and racism, two key factors in the development of the urban planning vocation. Again, this shows the importance of my proposed Africentric Sociourban Planning paradigm. In addition, these white folks also tend to selectively pick the pieces of history that make them (whites), as a race, appear to be nothing more than gifted scholars, planners, creators, innovators and developers who do what they do for everyone, as if there is no bias in what they think, say and do.

The preceding quote, the introduction to the article, is a prototypical example of this. Let me show you how and why.

Ms. Erikson begins by bringing up the first urban planning conference and how it was held in New York in 1898. Contextually speaking, let me give you a hint about what was going on in the United States at the time these white men were gathering around a table discussing the city and how to "plan" for it.

For one thing, according to the Census of 1990 (which of course, is really about the country's status in 1899), there were 75,994,575 people in the United States and of that number, 8,833,994 were black. That means that during that time of the urban planning meeting in New York, black people represented 11.6% of the total population. Where was our representation at this meeting? I'll tell you: an explanation is not necessary because in the world of the white revisionist historian, black people simply did not exist anywhere except the cotton field "down South." How else to explain such a glaring omission?

Secondly, the Spanish-American War began on April 21. Sixteen regiments of black volunteers were recruited; four saw combat. Five black Americans won

Congressional Medals of Honor. And since the . Founded on September 15, the National Afro-American Council elected Bishop Alexander Walters its first president, why weren't they invited to the meeting or consulted? My point is that race was certainly a social factor. It would have been in my sociourban paradigm. And we cannot forget that in November of that year (November 10), in Wilmington, North Carolina, eight black Americans were killed during white rioting.

Third, it would seem that being concerned about the "urban areas" would mean being concerned about what was taking place around the nation as it relates to a population that you are aware of (blacks). In 1898, 101 black people were known to have been lynched and 85 more were lynched in 1999. In 1900, 106 more black people were lynched. Did this group of men who were "planning" not care about these social facts? Or were black people deemed too "irrelevant" to even give a care about?

Fourth and finally, The Wilmington Insurrection of 1898, also known as the Wilmington Massacre of 1898 or the Wilmington Race Riot of 1898.This is a riot that occurred in Wilmington, North Carolina on November 10, 1898 and following days; it is considered a turning point in North Carolina politics following Reconstruction. New York surely got the news and the planners surely found out about it. What steps did they take? I ask this question because it will serve as a necessary foundation for a point that Ms. Erikson will make later in this analysis.

It was in the year 1898, New York consolidated five contiguous cities into one great city of five boroughs: Manhattan (also known as New York City), The Bronx, Queens, Brooklyn and Staten Island.(Soul of America, 2012). All this was taking place under the banner of urban growth and development, but there was no mention of the black community or any people of color whatsoever. Erikson (2012) claims, and correctly so, that,

> Before then, there were three types of people thinking about how
> a city should look and function — architects, public health
> officials, and social workers. Each group approached the question
> of city building very differently (Erikson, 2012).

All three groups of people were white and therefore no one else was really given any consideration. I am sharing this with you because the allegations I make against the urban planning discipline sound harsh. But it is always better to deal with hard, cold facts that pleasant, but unproductive dreams. The three groups of people mentioned above are then broken down by Erikson, like so:

> **The architects** were focused on the city as a built environment,
> implementing ideas like L'Enfant's grand vision for Washington,

> D.C., and the New York City grid (set out by the Commissioner's Plan of 1811). **The public health professionals**, on the other hand, were consumed with infrastructure. They knew there was a connection between certain diseases and social conditions, even if they didn't know precisely what it was … And lastly the **social workers** wanted to use the city to improve the lives of the people living there. They wanted cleaner tenements, spaces for immigrant children to play, and more light and fresh air for residents (Erikson, 2012 – emphasis added).

Architects are concerned with building the environment based on white people's needs and desires. Until public housing came into being many years later, that was just the way it was: housing and skyscrapers for white folks and black people could fight it out in the slums and other hazard-filled areas of the city. The public health professionals were concerned with water, lights and preventing the rise in disease, which was all the more reason to confine the elements that would give rise to disease (contaminated water, diseased trees) to areas of the city where white people didn't frequent.

And third, the fact that social workers were present. The claim is that they wanted cleaner tenements, spaces of immigrant children to play and fresh air – all within the segregated spaces that were laid out. For instance, instead of working to eliminate the need for tenements and low income housing (providing jobs and the like), it is easier to teach the poor to "suffer peacefully." That's what Malcolm X was speaking about in his "Message to the Grass Roots" many years later:

> It's like when you go to the dentist, and the man's going to take your tooth. You're going to fight him when he starts pulling. So he squirts some stuff in your jaw called novocaine, to make you think they're not doing anything to you. So you sit there and 'cause you've got all of that novocaine in your jaw, you suffer peacefully. Blood running all down your jaw, and you don't know what's happening. 'Cause someone has taught you to suffer -- peacefully.

This process of pacification is alive and well and apparent in nearly every American institution that has something to do with or interacts with black people. And so it would come to be up to this day and age where police kill black men in the streets and uncle tom preachers are marched out to organize prayer vigils and public protests to show and promote "suffering peacefully."

Continuing with the article on the history of urban planning:

> These thinkers were brought together by the pressure cooker that was the Industrial Revolution. "At that moment, we began to look for technological ways to expand the city," says <u>Elliott Sclar</u>, a

professor of urban planning at Columbia University. "All of a sudden here's a pressure to comprehensively plan. You can't just put a privy wherever you want." (Erikson, 2012).

That is not true. The goal was to "put a privy wherever you wanted" but to disguise the fact that this was what you were going to do. The Industrial Revolution meant that upgrades in the streets and transportation could spread cities out and make them larger. But that space didn't apply to black people. Black people were compartmentalized in those slums and tenements alluded to earlier and all that space and greenery (and later parks and waterways) were for the aesthetic and health-related leisure and pleasure of white folks.

The streets were very important consideration because they would pave the way for increased transportation arteries. But first things first:

> In 1898, the question of the hour was horse manure. City streets were just covered in the stuff, and there were no easy answers in sight. **Horses, after all, were the key mode of transportation in cities at the time.** At this initial meeting, fledgling planners realized that cities needed big plans to deal with growing populations. (Erikson, 2012 – emphasis added).

The streets were filled with horse shit which made side walks and porch like accommodations all the more important. Livery stables had to be constructed to make sure that the horses were shod and had a place to stay when people came to town. But the priorities of these planners was construction and expansion – building around the problem. That is why,

> At that conference, and in the years that followed, any one of these early urban planning strains could have taken over as the intellectual giant in the field. Though the social workers and the public health officials continued to play a role, urban planning's intellectual history ended up grounded in architecture (Erikson, 2012).

The priority was then as it is now: build, build, build. These white folks want to expand their territory by building into it. That is how the suburbs and exurbs came into being. The social problems, including the public works issues, remained while the buildings kept coming up. Land use was about to take a formal position in the white man's on-going landgrabbing, having already been started as he murdered off First Nation people and fenced in whatever properties he wanted as "his own." My allegations about the need for the ASP paradigm rests in the fact that white people did not want to address any concerns that black people, migrating north from the south, might have. And the schools played a part in that myopic thinking:

> That outcome is thanks in a large part to the creation of the country's first urban planning school, at Harvard. The University founded a school of **landscape architecture in 1898**. It was, effectively, **a vanity project**, slavishly devoted to Frederick Law Olmstead (in fact, it was started by Olmstead's son). At the same time, It was a place to start. **Soon after, they began offering classes in city planning, a first for higher education in America** (Erikson, 2012 – emphasis added).

You can see what the priorities were from the get-go: landscape. That basically means land and the control of the land. It means the shaping of the land to accommodate the growing white presence. Olmstead was mostly concerned about using "space" for white leisure. In fact, to this day it is Olmstead who is considered "the father of American landscape architecture." Urban planning would come much later.

White men were calling the shots as can be seen in the following description of the Harvard approach to planning:

> "You couldn't separate the design of the land from the design of the city," says Anthony Alofsin, who wrote *The Struggle for Modernism*, on the history of Harvard's urban planning school. At the beginning, the school focused on architectural history, with professors working at the city planning school along with the school of architecture and the school of landscape design. **"These faculty were interchangeable, it was very collaborative,"** Alofsin says (Erikson, 2012 – emphasis added).

The section I have emphasized above – the concept of interchangeable and collaborative faculty – is the key to white supremacy in higher education. That "I'll-wash-your-hands-you-wash-mine" approach has been a part of education in general for centuries. They stand in the classroom and quote their white predecessors and dub them "the father" of this or "the originator" of that. They maintain their system until a new white man comes along to offer new information and insights. Urban Planning was no different. What they are referring to as "architecture" is really white creativity with the resources to build run amok. There may have been initiative and ingenuity involved, but all those buildings, monuments and other structures shared one thing: that was the sign that would be attached that read, "no niggers allowed."

What I call "land grabbing" is re-worded in the following excerpt:

America's first city planners were very influenced by this focus on
physical space. "The first graduates were trained as designers,"
Alofsin says. "These were not policy wonks - they got hired by
cities to make plans." And plan they did. It was from these early
classes that the first crop of true city-affiliated planners were
born. (Erikson, 2012).

"The focus on physical space." That's a nice way to put coming into a
situation and murdering off the native population, placing those you didn't kill on
"reservations" and then divvying up the land among your race members by
offering "free land" to whites across the water to "come on over" and grab yourself
a chunk of earth! There were "land runs" and contests held to go parcel off some
land, a point driven home in the 1992 Tom Cruise movie, "Far and Away,"
described in the snippets as follows: "A young Irish couple flee to the States, but
subsequently struggle to obtain land and prosper freely."

The Indian Removal Act had already been passed in 1830, and that paved
the way of "clearing the way" for the white immigrants to make their move. So
when the historials like Erikson euphemize what took place as a "focus on physical
space," they don't talk about the "sociourban" realities the way the ASP paradigm
would do. That land acquisition was about theft, murder and a lot of bloodshed
regardless of the sterilized activity taking place in higher education:

> The advent of urban-conscious planners meant that cities began to
> create their own master plans. Harland Bartholomew, the famed
> city planning consultant, prepared comprehensive or master plans
> for dozens communities in the early 20th century, including
> Memphis, Newark, New Jersey, and <u>Columbus, Ohio</u>. (Erikson,
> 2012).

The point that should be understood from the following passage is that this
was a collective effort based on race and vision. At no time did a single one of
these white "Christians" have anything to say about including black people in the
overall improvement of the lives of their fellow whites. Even the ethnics who had
staggered over here from across the water were given consideration, and that
consideration was based on race.

The endemic race-based visions of these white men who helped give form
and function to today's urban planning can be seen in the following excerpt:

> As Stuart Meck, a professor of urban planning at Rutgers
> explains, cities used urban planning not to build better, or cleaner,
> or morally uplifting cities. They used planners to divide the city,
> creating beautiful spaces at the expense of the poor. (Erikson,
> 2012).

In Euroamerican culture, the descriptors "clean," "pure," and "good" are all synonyms for the word "white." And as you just read, that is what urban planners wanted their world to be. They considered their white nationalistic views, based on land appropriated from First Nation people, as "morally uplifting." And in "dividing the city," they did so along racial and class lines, more of the former than the latter. And as they must admit, all of this came "at the expense of the poor."

The reason why that latter point is mentioned is because it is so obvious, so plainly visible, that to acknowledge that robbing the poor took place is as normal as saying the sky is blue. They knew what they were doing but the people they were robbing didn't have political power. Furthermore, once you get out of enslavement and decide to head North, the last thing you want to do is get settled and then start raising hell about not liking the accommodations!

Stuart Meck, the man quoted earlier, is alleged to have made the following statement:

> In an email, he writes:
> **City planning, along with zoning, was a vehicle to control where African-Americans, the poor, and immigrants lived, and to keep them out of the areas where middle and upper class people resided.** It is no coincidence that the initial efforts to adopt land use controls in the U.S. were aimed at **enacting racial zoning—zoning that segregated cities by race.** The first city to adopt racial zoning was Baltimore in 1910, **and racial zoning spread to other eastern and southern cities** (e.g., Atlanta, Louisville), even though the U.S. Supreme Court declared it unconstitutional in **1917, in a case titled Buchanan v. Warley.** (Erikson, 2012 – emphasis added).

Yet another after the fact explanation of the racism that existed long enough for the system to be set up. Once that's done it's easy to talk about what used to be – as if that is truly the case. The claim that racial zoning was declared unconstitutional in *Buchanan v. Warley* doesn't mean any more than the fact that Jim Crow laws were ruled unconstitutional in the *Brown v. Board of Education* decision in 1954. De facto racism trumps de jure discrimination and that is why the urban planners are still segregating, still working with banking interests to "steer" and redline, and communities are still being gerrymandered.

This short history and the corrects made to it herein, provide the facts and foundations on which to accept and work toward implementing the ASP paradigm with all deliberate speed. That is the only way change will begin to take place. As the Cameroon proverb teaches, "The stream won't be advised, therefore its course is crooked." And that is the way urban planning continues to exist: by rejecting positive and productive input from those that it systematically oppresses.

Central City PREDATORS: How Lenders, Housing Manipulators and Segregation Makes America Rich

INTRODUCTION

The lyrics by Ice-T and Ice Cube from the 1992 movie "Trespass" pretty much sum up the black reaction to what I am about to describe in this paper:

> How many bullets can your back hold, suckin' from the H-K
> The red dot's on your dome, from the light ray
> Boom bam bust oh shit kid, your head is a pile of puss
> I'm kickin' up much dust, the nigga ya can't trust
> **This is my shit, my hood, my turf**
> **My gold, my grip, whatever the fuck it's worth**
> I don't need nobody comin' in my territory
> tryin' to rip a nigga off and fuck your fuckin' sob stories
> Take a good look at my motherfuckin' jacker
> **About to feel the wrath, of a greedy ass cracker**
> Pale as snow, so you know the hoe stand out
> **Comin' in my hood with his hand out**
> Tryin' to get over on the black, but the motherfuckin' mack
> will put a fuckin' slug in his back
> And with the boom ping ping, it ain't no thing to blast
> on greedy motherfuckers that trespass (emphasis added)

What are the lyrics referring to in terms of metaphorical relevance?

In most cities in the United States, cowardly old white men in suits and ties sit around a table interlaced with a few water-carrying "negroes" who sit silently while these white men concoct new and ingenious ways to control the inner cities, be they Black or Mexican. In most cases these actions take place in urban planning departments or perhaps in the mayor's "office of community development."

These actions take place by using Federal dollars, secured after they (the white men known as "city planners") pledge t use the free moneyto improve and develop those "low-income areas. This has been going on since 1974 – 44 years – and there has been very little improvement to speak of in those low-income areas.

The money is spent on suburban expansion, annexation, downtown development, parks and recreation and the hiring of other white folks who can lend their energy and effort to maintaining this state of affairs.

The urban planners and their "master plans" pave the way for the encroachment that takes place for the benefit of white folks and at the detriment of people of color.

RACIAL MEANINGS OF HOUSING

A 2012 article by Evelyn Wyly and others titled, "New Racial Meanings of Housing in America" that appeared in the September 2012 issue of *American Quarterly*, shall serve as the basis for my analysis of the housing situation in Omaha's black community and the central city predators who, even now, are working in the name of "redevelopment" to take over the black community's land and housing stock, relocate the indigenous population, and re-enter the area which is close to the airport, the riverfront, downtown jobs and the flattest land in the city. What is going on in Omaha is taking place in cities all over America, from Houston and New Orleans to the California Bay Area and the east coast.

Housing is an important consideration because it is a reflection of the quality of life of a people, of a neighborhood, of entire communities. To control the housing stock is to control the people who live in and depend on that housing. That is "the key to the colors," as the late Dr. Frances Cress Welsing would put it. And urban planners and their colleagues – contractors, developers, banking and lending interests and city and county officials – are all in on the use of housing control to dictate the fate, future and configuration of black communities all over the nation. Omaha then, is but one.

Urban planning is about land use and land controls in a given city or area. With people in control who are of one racial background, the end result and "vision" is always going to be one that favors that racial grouping. All that other groups can expect is compartmentalization, segregation, high population density, selective neglect, and various forms of segregation.

The article on the "meanings of housing," written by Wyly, et al. (2012) begins thusly:

> Ideals of housing and home have always shaped periods of social
> and political transformation in America … For more than a century
> these ideals have been intertwined with segregation and the
> structured inequalities of capital and race … Challenges to class
> inequality and racism have been repeatedly deflected and co-opted
> by the complex social and political construct of the "American
> Dream" of home ownership.

The challenges have been deflected and co-opted because the people who were trying to expose the racism and cheating, the people who were working to overturn the discrimination, were foolishly making moral appeals to immoral people. They were, as Malcolm X would have said, "running from the wolf to the fox." They were expecting to make a case against Jesse James by appealing to the judgment of his brother, Frank James. The fact is, *institutions are designed to perpetuate systems, not condemn them.* So the housing control remains in the hands of white urban planners, bankers, developers and city planners while black people, for the most part, remain powerless in a nation where power is valued above all else.

Continuing:

> We should not be surprised, therefore, that the worst financial crisis since the Great Depression of the 1930s has destabilized the social relations of racial categories and identities in America's ongoing drama of racial formation … For decades, the simultaneous acceleration of privatization and debt allowed white privilege to ignore Derrick Bell's call "to 'Get Real' about race and racism in America," to deal honestly with "the increasingly dismal demographics that reflect the status of those whose forebears in this country were slaves … (Wyly, et. al., 2012)

Several flaws are evident in the previous paragraph, one that is laden with homespun racist assumptions and metaphysical interpretations of reality.

First the claim that the financial crisis "destabilized the social relations of racial categories and identities." That has never been the case. No matter how bad the economic situation in America has been, white folks have always maintained their racist beliefs. Most of them would abandon Christianity before they would even consider abandoning their beliefs in white supremacy. There may be Great Depressions, recessions and other economic problems, but that red, white and blue flag is more than a piece of cloth to the American racist. It is a way of life that doesn't have much room to practice or promote cultural competency or cultural relativity.

Secondly, the claim that it was white privilege that led to ignoring the realities of race and racism in America. White privilege was a component of it, but what enabled whites to ignore "getting real" with issues of race was psychological preservation and racial ego. Without that, white privilege would be of little use. White privilege is the support beam that holds white supremacy together. And urban planners use the physicality of the environment to put into visualization the existence of the white supremacy that these people claim is justified as a basis for their rule.

Third, and an extension of number two is the claim that the ignoring of those racial realities led to America dealing honestly with "the the increasingly dismal demographics that reflect the status of those whose forebears in this country were slaves …" Again, we have to look at the role of urban planning: the ultimate definer of social and geographic reality. As would be pointed out in the ASP paradigm, culture is the basis of all ideas, images and actions. It is white cultural values and their power to impose that paves the way for decisions in all institutions that support the system, and that includes the area of housing and urban development.

Urban planning is more than pencils, charts and maps. The discipline, as you can see through the Harvard School, works hand-in-hand with various forms of economic development for the purpose of social control. If racial segregation did not make America rich, there would have been no racial segregation, plain and simple. As noted by Wyly,

> Housing—and especially the expansion of mortgage debt—was crucial in deflecting the more fundamental demands for redistribution and genuine economic justice that grew out of the civil rights movement. Risky, deceptive practices in the "subprime" mortgage market were particularly effective in replacing the old rigid justifications for **exclusionary** racism with more flexible, entrepreneurial forms of **inclusionary** discrimination that promised opportunity and access to the wonders of the market. The American Dream: no money down! (Wyly, et. al., 2012 – emphasis added)

By engaging in at risk subprime lending, those in power could extend loans to people not qualified to repay them. Then they could repossess the housing and ruin the credit of the borrower at the same time. So if the end result was racist control and domination, the end result was achieved. Include the oppressed in their own state of degradation and there is no need to exclude them from the system because their very presence in the system as debtors, borrowers and losers of housing helps justify the stigma, helps perpetuate reasoning for denying them in the first place, and makes the system look as if "we tried but those people just can't get it."

Furthermore,

> **Predatory home-financing schemes were perfected in subaltern America**, among the people and places marginalized by social relations of class, race/ethnicity, gender, and metropolitan spatial

> restructuring. For years, well-documented cases of targeting and predatory exploitation were waved away by policy elites as "anecdotal." High-profile legislative and regulatory debates typically featured economists and U.S. senators—**almost always white men**— sternly assuring everyone that **the free market was delivering widespread benevolence** and that we should not worry too much about these **isolated cases**. (Wyly, et. al., 2012 – emphasis added)

Let me take time to add several points of correction and clarification of some of the statements made in the previous excerpt.

The use of the term "subaltern" is just another way of saying "lower class." The white man keeps track of these class distinctions which is one reason for the Census. He knows where the poor live, how they are housed and as a result of both of these, what he can do to interject the variable of "race" into home ownership, which most people refer to as "The American Dream."

Secondly, of course it's almost always white men. And the use of the term "almost" is for social courtesy. It is ALWAYS the white man because it is his system. Even when a few negroes or "coons" are allowed to have decision making positions regarding predatory loans, they got those jobs because they have shown that they will obey their marching orders and act in the same way a white man would act and to treat black and brown applicants with the same chicanery that the Anglo would.

Third, the myth that the free market will deliver widespread deliverance is a myth, not so much to dupe blacks (who know better) but to convince witless and naïve whites that America is truly a land of equality. If the myth of "widespread benevolence" can be circulated, then white people – voters – can be pacified. It doesn't matter how you define that "benevolence." Let me give you an example before moving on.

There is what I call "the Toys for Tots Syndrome." Almost every major city has one, and it takes place around Christmas time. This is a program along with others like "Coats for Kids" and "Back to School Giveaways." All of these programs target children and provide them with toys, coats or backpacks, whatever they need. This is done with the assistance of their parents who witness these acts as being examples of "widespread benevolence," no doubt. But what is really happening is that a system of paternalistic racism is established because by doling out all this consumable bullshit, you control the masses, the books, backpacks and toys are eventually destroyed and then it's back to begging the following year. In other words, the system of leeching and dependency perpetuates itself. This is the only kind of "widespread benevolence" these crackers are talking about.

And the cheating and the victims being "isolated cases," this is true in a way. If you are using the term "isolated" as a way of saying that these cases will be kept away from every happening to members of the mainstream, then you are correct. But what is meant by these white people is that these "isolated" cases only happen every once in a while and that there is therefore no reason to worry. Can you see the difference? And the gullible American public will opt for the more palatable definition, the one that best buttresses the "widespread benevolence" claims, and then get on about their business.

Moving right along we find the case of Trayvon Martin:

> … Several years later, another gun was fired. This time it was not self-inflicted, but a gunshot motivated by another person, with (1) a deep desire to protect a community where the housing crisis has frayed the social fabric, (2) an in-your-face personality sharpened by several encounters with law enforcement, (3) a suspicion of young black men, or (4) some combination of all factors. (Wyly, et. al., 2012).

The fact is, all this already existed and has existed ever since black migration from the South to the North. White men, in general, fear black men, in general. And it is from this reality that the previous excerpt is based, not on the lone and tragic case of the February 26, 2012 shooting of Trayvon Martin:

> Seventeen-year-old Trayvon Martin was walking back from a convenience store to the home where his father was staying with his fiancée, **in a gated community just outside Orlando, Florida**. George Zimmerman, twenty-eight, saw Trayvon and called 911; Zimmerman was the coordinator for **the neighborhood watch** in the Retreat at Twin Lakes, where property values have fallen by half since the new community was completed six years ago; **"a 'significant number' of foreclosures . . . have prompted investors to buy the properties at a discount and then rent them out …** (Wyly, et. al., 2012 – emphasis added).

So let's deal contextually with the issue of "race in housing" and not use selective or individualized incidents to make the case. White historians have a tendency to do that to deflate and deflect the traditional and long-term evil that they have perpetrated upon an entire society and the world. The fact is, white flight led to the idea for these "new developments" and white fear was the reason for the "gated communities", communities that came along with security guards.

Continuing on:

> Zimmerman told the 911 dispatcher he was concerned about recent
> break-ins, **"and there's a real suspicious guy."** Zimmerman
> ignored the dispatcher's instructions to wait for the police, and
> **chased down Trayvon**; a struggle ensued, and the unarmed teen
> was shot dead. After persuading the police he acted in self-defense,
> Zimmerman was released. Indignant rage spread quickly—an
> unarmed boy was dead, and no one was even arrested—until a
> special prosecutor filed second-degree murder charges. (Wyly, et.
> al., 2012)

What few said anything about was that Zimmerman was a man of color to an extent. But he had learned his lessons well, just like those loan officers who may have skin color but who follow the corporate script and engage in predator lending anyway. Zimmerman's case became a housing issue in the following way:

> Public debate focused on Zimmerman's identity, biography, and
> **racial attitudes: a Catholic altar boy** whose father was a U.S.
> Army intelligence veteran of the Vietnam War and whose mother
> was a **Peruvian immigrant**. After high school graduation,
> Zimmerman moved to Florida and became a real estate broker as the
> market flourished. He was making more than $10,000 a month by
> his early twenties, but when the market collapsed he held a series of
> service-sector jobs before landing a full-time position at a "fraud-
> detection company," Digital Risk, that "helps institutions like Bank
> of America and Freddie Mac **to rid their balance sheets of the
> kinds of toxic loans that led to the 2008 banking crisis.** Mr.
> Zimmerman was among hundreds of auditors who work in a four-
> story office building . . . **mining borrowers' files, sniffing out lies
> and scrutinizing hardship letters ...** (Wyly, et. al., 2012 –
> emphasis added)

Some say "tragic accident," I say "perfect storm." Again, the contextualist approach makes it clear.

First of all, a Catholic. As quiet as it's kept, Catholics have contributed major damage to black history and black life. It was a Catholic priest, Father Bartolome Las Casas, who recommended going to Africa and enslaving blacks to bring back to work in the cotton fields of the South. It was a Catholic, Chief Justice Roger Taney, who ruled in the case of Plessy v. Ferguson (1896) that, "A black man has no rights a white man is bound to respect." Know this latter instance, fast forward to 2012 and Trayvon Martin: from 1896 to 2012 the same mentality is pervasive, both held by Catholic trained men. After 116 years, a black man still had no rights a white man was bound to respect.

Secondly, Zimmerman's mother was a Peruvian immigrant meaning that she was a woman of color, and if you look at photos of him, you can see that he was

Hispanic. But as Karenga (1967) wrote, "White doesn't represent a color; it represents a mentality that is anti-black." Zimmerman had his fears based on his job, which was to cast doubt on the borrowers of those loans, most of whom were people of color. This brings us to point number three.

What do you think his job description translates to mean when the author writes that Zimmerman's job was, "to rid their balance sheets of the kinds of toxic loans that led to the 2008 banking crisis"? If these people had hound dogs, shot guns and moved in a pack they would be the modern day version of the "slave hunters" of old.

Point number four proves it: poor people are guilty until proven innocent. Put another way, Zimmerman's job consisted of, "mining borrowers' files, sniffing out lies and scrutinizing hardship letters." Guilty until proven innocent because the on-going loan problems had to be put on someone. A convenient scapegoat would be the borrowers of color and those who were poor. And that's what Zimmerman's REAL job was and it shaped his attitude about how to act and react whenever he saw skin color. Race and housing – all given form and function by a system whose key urban planning personnel paved the way for the separatism and discrimination that was to follow.

The system had it all figured out, from application to public relations. For instance as an example of the latter,

> A despondent elderly black women is alone in her bedroom, blaming herself for borrowing too much from the nation's largest mortgage lender, described by its cofounder and CEO as "having **helped 25 million people buy homes** and prevented social unrest by extending loans to minorities, historically the victims of discrimination… (Wyly, et. al., 2012).

What is the message? "We better get these niggas some housing or they'll burn the country down the way they did in the '60s." But this time around money had to be made up front. So they started lending money to unqualified applicants and covering it up as if it was a "mercy flirt." They "helped' 25 people buy homes the same way that the farmer is "helping" the mule stay in shape by working it in the fields and treating it as a beast of burden. The social unrest was "by minorities," you'll also note and the reason for the anticipation is that they had been victims of housing discrimination before. In other words, the white man was doing low-income and minorities a favor with their loan programs.

But as the saying teaches, "Anticipation of death is worse than death itself." This society wasn't going to take any chances as housing discrimination charge after housing discrimination charge mounted up.

Look how Trayvon's plight is used as a promotional tool:

> A young black teen is profiled as **"young, loitering, non-property owning and poor,"** and shot by the vigilant protector of a Sun Belt suburban gated community, **a man who knows the importance of surveillance, real estate, and property values** … "Welcome to gate-minded America … where **"an 'us vs. them' mentality festers"** and property values are sustained "by creating an external enemy—**those people outside the walls** … (Wyly, et. al., 2012 – emphasis added)

Again, once we contextualize the issue of housing and race we can see that what was just described had already existed in the minds of white folks and had been carried out during enslavement. Blacks owned no property and if you weren't "owned" by someone you were deemed a "runaway," which translates to mean "loiterer." And as today, during enslavement the man who "knew the importance of surveillance, real estate and property values" was not only the plantation owner, but the small white farmer as well. Jealousy over the fact that their southern brothers had Africans working the cotton fields while they (the northerners) didn't was one of the reasons for the civil war.

The "us versus them" mentality existed the minute the African dropped his first loin cloth in front of a European visitor. That was what set it all off. Charles Stember (*Sexual Racism: The Emotional Barrier to an Integrated Society*, 1978), Joel Kovel (*White Racism: A Psychohistory*, 1984) and Calvin C. Hernton (*Sex and Racism in America*, 1992) make it clear that all this institutional and individual hatred has to do with the white male's own deep-seated feelings of sexual inadequacy. And this means that those "outside the walls" means the "walls of skin color," where white is at the top of the hierarchy.

> These stories demand a reconsideration of American racial and ethnic relations—and in particular, changes in the connection between individual experiences of discrimination and the wider structures of inequality in American housing … **The predatory exploitation of the urban core has gone mainstream, altering the spatial relations of privilege on the expanding frontiers of Sun Belt suburbia …** (Wyly, et. al., 2012 – emphasis added)

Even when white scholars attempt to "come clean" with their history – in this case an explanation of the racialization of housing – they cannot quite bring themselves to do it – the burden of the cultural super-ego is just too much to bear. So they engage in partial truth telling. Take, for example, the previous statement that, "The predatory exploitation of the urban core has gone mainstream, altering the spatial relations of privilege on the expanding frontiers of Sun Belt suburbia …" The key is in the qualifier "has gone mainstream."

Predatory exploitation of the slums, the ghetto, the urban core – whatever you want to call it – has taken place ever since these locales were established by way of racial segregation and discrimination. Why else would they exist? The white man has to make money off of his discriminatory acts or else it will cost him more money to maintain them than they are worth. The concept of predatory lending may rather relatively new, but predatory exploitation is as old as the (white) predators themselves.

Background information continues:

> A generation ago, John S. Adams and other housing analysts suggested that postindustrialism was eroding the old foundations of scarcity—ending the long period of easy speculative real estate gains delivered through the steady suburbanization of the modern industrial metropolis … **The information economy would erode the arbitrage opportunities of geography, history, and urbanization**. Housing would no longer promise to make everyone rich … **but would instead become a partly decommodified realm governed by the socially necessary use values of home, neighborhood, and community** (Wyly, et. al., 2012 – emphasis added)

What specialists like Wyly don't seem to understand is the EFFECT of the economy on the poor. It matters not what the process or procedures are. The society can be in a state of post-industrialization or an "information age" type culture: the white man is going to do what white people do. Acquire, horde, exploit and engage in the ceaseless pursuit of profit. It's really no more complex than that.

The information economy is a derivative of the post-industrial economy! It is the offspring of the advent of the giant corporation, the factor and other components. Like the post-industrial society, the information society also is a shift from manufacturing and focuses on new science-based industries using the computer, the internet and various web sites. Like the post –industrial society, the information society also relies on the rise of new principles of stratification, meaning that there is no longer the upper-, middle and lower class workers, but now there are two main strata: rich and poor. This is the kind of "change" that Silicon Valley and others have ushered in.

In June of 2018 it was reported that the three richest men in the world, for the first time, came from the tech field. They are Jeff Bezos of Amazon.com (and also owner of the Washington Post), Mark Zuckerberg of Facebook and Bill Gates of Microsoft. The gap between the rich and poor, what the social scientists refer to as a "pay disparity," is widening more than it ever has during the times of post-industrialism.

Nothing has been "de-commodified." These white people and their commodity society are more intent than ever to reducing everything, from housing and the furniture in it, to the people who sit in that house and on that furniture to commodities. And within that realm human beings are viewed in one of two ways: as tangible assets or as crippling liabilities.

The "scam" was on, and this time with the advent of computers and the coming of social media, it was easier to locate a powerless demographic and target them. But first, you had to upgrade the technology needed to make the scam one that would work on a mass scale:

> **Adams and his colleagues could not have predicted the speed and power of neoliberal policy decisions in the 1980s and 1990s that created a "global circulation of mortgages" that transformed local housing into "an electronic instrument** ... as the local lives and needs of individual home owners making monthly payments became the "postindustrial widgets" of mortgage-backed securities ... (Wyly, et. al., 2012 – emphasis added)

What you just read could possibly be bullshit. The speed and power of neoliberal policy can be predicted because the people doing the predicting are the ones who helped shape the conditions for it! These white men and their greed are always the motivating factors for these types of changes and they realize that such changes are inevitable. With greed comes need for more speed – to bleed the gullible American public of its human capital potential and to translate it, by any means necessary, into working revenue streams.

Another debate issue on race and housing follows:

> Housing-related debt was only part of the broader financialization of the American economy—before the collapse, the financial sector accounted for more than two-fifths of all U.S. corporate profits— **but risky mortgage lending was a crucial site of innovation and exploitation that connected local inequalities with global circuits of investment, risk, and speculation** (Wyly, et. al., 2012 – emphasis added)

The fact is "local inequalities and global circuits of investment, risk and speculation were ALWAYS connected. How could they not be? The motivator, creator and monitor of both spheres – local inequality and the global variables mentioned – are one and the same. Both share the same banking interests and both attend the same financial meetings. Both read the same reports and both seek the profits and revenue streams of big business. Consider local inequality the battery that starts the car with the global aspect being the engine. Both are different but nevertheless inseparably bound and interdependent. They are not mutually exclusive.

The following passage provides some semblance of evidence of what I just postulated:

> Postmaterialist interpretations of housing reflected broader debates over the nature of postindustrial society and were quickly subsumed within the economic theorists' view of a world freed from the messy constraints of real-world geographies… These visions guided key policy decisions on banking deregulation for an entire generation … deregulated market innovation reconfigured the relations between local housing markets and transnational financial circuits. **Preexisting local racisms were integrated into wider spatial networks.** But the insatiable "appetite for yield" enabled a ruinous …] competition that now threatens to undermine the political foundations of America's racial state … (Wyly, et. al., 2012 – emphasis added)

See? "Pre-existing local racisms (sic) were integrated into widier spatial networks." Those networks were global! The use of the term "racisms" implies that there is more than one. Racism is an umbrella ideology created for and by the white race, the race that directs racism through impositions and institutional arrangements. As Emerson made clear, a point that I will reiterate at the conclusion of this book, is "an institution is the length and shadow of a man." Racism is an institutional arrangement that is global in its impact. There need not be two or three of them because racism functions to benefit the white race in all of its forms. The only functioning racism in the known universe is white supremacy.

And it's based on race. Coming back home to the United States we find that,

> Between 2004 and 2006, Wall Street and local lenders funneled more than $20 billion in high-risk, high-cost subprime mortgage credit to consumers in the Las Vegas area. Compared with otherwise similar non-Hispanic whites, African American, and Latina/o borrowers in the region **were twice as likely to be pushed into subprime credit** (Wyly, et. al., 2012 – emphasis added).

As we can see, what was the criteria? It was skin color. And who was doing the deciding? The white man. Who is therefore responsible, the people who did the borrowing knowing their credit was bad, or the people in charge who spent countless hours marketing various programs, promoting the loans, pretending that they gave a damn and then hooking these people up with loans that they knew would and could not be rapid?

This is how modern racism works. Sure the lynch rope and police dogs are pulled out of the holster every now and then, but economic racism and toxic racism get the same result: the long-term harm of black folks. Once your credit and future are sabotaged, the urban planners can move in with claims of "coming to the rescue" and offer up another one of their vaunted "programs" or "projects," the way they did with urban renewal, Model Cities, Community Development Block Grants and Urban Development Block Grants.

It boils down to spacing, segregation and the system's control of both. Put another way,

> In America's utopia of spatial form, **housing markets are defined by a regime of spatial segregation that keeps the other at a safe distance to protect white property values ...** For many years, this regime was reproduced through **pervasive practices of segregation in development and neighborhood social relations ...** Yet the law and economics of housing finance were also crucial—particularly the division between "traditional" forms of closely regulated prime credit of white privilege and scarcity and its "nontraditional" others ... (Wyly, et. al., 2012 – emphasis added)

As I stated earlier, the past is prologue and the traditional forms of segregation do not end or subside; they are merely modified through the use of new policies and procedures that have the computers doing the work. In that way you can reach (dupe) larger groups of people, promote the message at a faster rate, and rake in the profits and foreclose much quicker.

It's a matter of process, as is explained the following passage:

> At first, this other entailed **systematic exclusion from the institutions of mainstream credit.** Over time, however, **more and more marginalized people and places were incorporated into an expanding field of high-risk subprime and predatory debt ...** The expansion of debt in turn fueled an **acceleration in home prices, encouraging further innovations in leveraged risk—** generating **a steady stream of fees and investment returns for everyone in the industry ...** (Wyly, et. al., 2012 – emphasis added)

Important articles, regardless of error, are written the way they are written in order to get past the editors of these publications, in this case the American Quarterly – a highly touted magazine that only university professors read because urban planners don't read anything unless it has the word "urban" in it. So this information that exposes the scam is written in terms that few people can understand and, when coupled with the low readership of the journal, few people find out or can provide evidence about what is going on.

But I can.

The previous excerpt essentially lays out the scam from beginning to end. First cut off conventional credit after you sabotage the financial well-being of the people who apply for it. Once that's done it becomes a simple "bait-and-switch"; they come in and get rejected but "a-hah, we found something else that you might benefit from." And out comes the bullshit loan, the subprime mortgage application. You are asked to spread the word, that in addition to the fact that key people in your community have been asked if they can sponsor a seminar or a forum so you can share "the new program" with the other "marginalized people." That means ministers, community center operators and managers of elderly housing and nursing homes.

That's what is meant above by "expanding field." More people hear about and fall for the okey-doke – the way we do everything else in the black community (like "Christianity," for instance). Debt begins to rise as more people can't pay the loans back and as the debt rises, here come the new revenue streams: debt collection, foreclosures and the taking of property. People are evicted and forced into rental properties. Entire communities are cleaned out and the housing is re-sold for a fraction of its worth.

And who benefits? The real estate market:

> "Nontraditional" forms of credit became an ever more important source of income for *local* realtors, mortgage brokers, and appraisers, for *regional and national* banks and bank holding companies, and for Wall Street investment houses and investors around the world lured by the promise of high risk-adjusted yields. **But yields require volume** (Wyly, et. al., 2012 – emphasis added)

In other words, since the yields are such a high risk, it takes more "victims" to be able to justify the revenue stream. And that's where people of color, in droves, come in. So the key all along was to find a target market that was expendable and disposable. That meant people of color. Then hunker down and target them by providing them with loans that were high risk. This is what Warren Buffett did to the Native Americans in Gallup, New Mexico and Seattle, Washington. (For more on that read my book, *American Kleptocracy: Historical Examples, Present-Day Evidence and Real-World Application*).

These are reasons for my proposed Africentric Sociourban Planning paradigm is important. Knowledge is power and as the saying teaches us, "my people are destroyed from lack of knowledge." Most of the people negatively impacted didn't find out what was taking place until it was much too late.

My paradigm is geared toward providing information and evidence that something new is needed, something far more humanistic and culturally competent than what exists now. If need be, it can be used to indict urban planners and city administrators the nation over for their complicity in what can only be viewed as a "race-based scam":

> The *rate* of exploitative profits has always been highest among the segregated and marginalized, but market volume is another matter: housing finance starkly illustrates Slavoj Žižek's parallax view. Between 2004 and 2010 high-risk subprime mortgages accounted for more than 39 percent of all mortgage loans made to single, non-Hispanic African American women—almost four times the share for non-Hispanic white male-female couples, and more than five times the rate for non-Hispanic Asian or Hawaiian/Pacific Islander traditional couples; **these disparities are reduced only somewhat when we account for African American women's lower incomes and other factors …** Yet **non-Hispanic whites remain a dominant plurality** even in the subprime market, accounting for 45.9 percent of the 10.9 million high-cost loans made in these years … (Wyly, et. al., 2012 – emphasis added)

Even their own statistics, as much as they are fudged, distorted or erased, indict the endemic racism of what they have done when it comes to blacks and the housing market. Remember how far this society has come since the days of antebellum slavery and how the communities have expanded and technological advancements have increased exponentially. And yet look at people of color as described in the previous paragraph: lost and left too weak to do anything but wander.

It is for these reasons that,

> From the perspective of marginalized communities, **it is impossible to ignore the deeply racialized and gendered dimensions of the subprime boom and today's foreclosure disaster.** Nationwide, foreclosure starts and serious delinquency rates in **predominantly minority neighborhoods are more than twice as bad as those in predominantly white communities …** (Wyly, et. al., 2012 – emphasis added)

To begin with it is not "impossible" to ignore the deeply rooted racialized dimensions of subprime loans booming and the subsequent foreclosure disaster. It's not impossible because it was set up to end up that way. It's not impossible because the only people who didn't notice it were the ones who were the victims of it. How could there otherwise be all this documentation, these numbers, these demographic statistics if the situation hadn't been noticed beforehand, during and afterwards? It was the COMMUNITY and the POPULATIONS that were ignored, not what was being done to them!

As a result, minority foreclosures are twice what they are for whites. Is that a coincidence? Is any "disparity" between the races in America a quirk or a coincidence? Of course not. It's all by design. This time around the designers are city administrations, local banking interests, real estate companies and of course, urban planners and their vaunted "master plans."

The victims saw what was taking place. But how about the perpetrators and the ones making all the money? According to Wyly,

> But a different view appears from the perspective of Wall Street and transnational investors. As the market accelerated between 2004 and 2005, the subprime share among single black women shot up from 36.2 percent to 52.4 percent, dwarfing the comparable rates among non-Hispanic white male-female couples (from 9.5 percent to 14.5 percent). Yet each percentage point increase in subprime share among single black women delivered fewer than 5,800 new customers—each one an opportunity for deceptive fees and charges on the front end and an ongoing stream of returns from leverage and speculation through securitization. (Wyly, et. al., 2012)

The fees and the charges generated untold profits for these banking and lending interests. And the loans kept coming, the marketing of them continued, and the people who were applying for them felt they were getting a good deal because their options were so few. And the whites with bad credit were an even more lucrative and therefore exploitable revenue stream: "By contrast, each percentage-point advance in subprime market share among non-Hispanic white couples delivered more than thirty-four thousand new prospects. (Wyly, et. al., 2012)

> By the time the global circulation of mortgages really took off in the first decade of the twenty-first century, America's most deeply marginalized communities—**mostly but not exclusively, inner-city and inner-suburban neighborhoods of non-Hispanic African Americans**—had been **thoroughly devastated by generations of various kinds of exploitative financial schemes** (Wyly, et. al., 2012 – emphasis added)

First they start off by relegating black people slum life. Then, we were promoted to dilapidated housing and a more formal ghetto life. But that wasn't even enough because as a resilient people, those outsiders were not happy seeing us persevere despite the oncoming urban attacks. They launched urban renewal and Model Cities and reconfigured our communities and when that wasn't enough they came up with the subprime lending scam, veiled in marketed claims of "wanting to help." And look at the black communities of America now: broken up, fractured, relocated into little pockets, but still poor enough to enable the city to qualify for Federal grant dollars, again buttressed by the lie of "wanting to help."

Our communities were relocated from the core to the urban fringe, which made it appear that progress was being made. But in reality, those new locations were just as in need of assistance and therefore in need of "lending assistance." As a result, "New volume for the newest forms of capitalist predation required new targets: suburbanizing African Americans and Latina/os, and eventually some of the traditional beneficiaries of America's institutions of Anglo white privilege" (Wyly, et. al., 2012)

Again, it was not the actual "suburbanization" of Blacks and Latinos directly. It was more like playing on the promises and pledges of potential suburbanization when, in reality, it was more like a relocation strategy aimed at the urban fringe. To these chronically poor people, even that was a step upward. But the subprime loans still sold nevertheless. The author uses the example of what took place in Cleveland, Ohio:

> Cleveland was once an American icon, **famous for making things.** Then it became famous for **deindustrialization, environmental catastrophe, and depopulation.** Then came the predatory lending boom. More than $5 billion in subprime loans were made in the Cleveland metropolitan area at the height of the boom; these high-cost loans were about five times more likely to be sold to Wall Street and other private investors than conventional prime loans. (Wyly, et. al., 2012 – emphasis added)

So the factories came and left and people went under. Out of desperation they were sold a bill of goods, "loans" that they felt would save the day. But these subprime loans only served to make Wall Street wealthy while the poor people who received them got nothing in return but poor credit, foreclosures and bankruptcy. As a result,

> Now the ongoing foreclosure crisis is making Cleveland famous yet again, this time for tearing down houses. Cleveland has about fifteen thousand vacant and abandoned homes, and dealing with them is described by the county land bank president as "the root canal of community development." Source: B Dennis, "The Foreclosure Crush," *Washington Post*, October 15, 2011. (Wyly, et. al., 2012)

Again we have more vacant lots and abandoned houses. The quote about such conditions being "the root canal of community development" sounds cute but it's not impacting on the "mouth" of white people. The root canal is in the mouth of the black community, which bears the brunt of the vermin creeping all over, and the hazards such as abuse of individuals who are harmed as deviants use the high weeds and vacant houses for hideaways. The city comes in every now and then and does some landscaping (mowing of yards and tree control), but they turn around and send the bill to the homeowner!

The racial situation in housing is rigged so that white people win even when they lose. For instance, note the following:

> White privilege in accumulated wealth enables most of these communities to better resist the devalorization of the ongoing crisis—foreclosure and delinquency rates are half those in the most racially marginalized and segregated neighborhoods—but volume again tells a different story. **Two-fifths of all foreclosure starts nationwide are in predominantly white neighborhoods** (Wyly, et. al., 2012 – emphasis added)

Again, we have a partial truth. The author(s) claim that 2/5 of all foreclosures nationwide are in predominantly white neighborhoods. But guess who they sell or better yet, rent those houses out to? Desperate minorities seeking to move into those neighborhoods. If they don't "get over" that way, they turn around and simply abandon the home and along comes the realtor to put it on the auction block and try to make back as much of the money as he can. Since the credit of the homeowner is screwed anyway, what does he/she care if they are charged with leaving the house behind? This is a white nation and one way or the other the white man is going to figure out a way to place the blame, the debt, the service fees, the negative credit rating – on some individual or group of people of color.

Time moves on but race relations remain the same for the most part. For instance,

> **It is now widely recognized that the stable, locally oriented "golden age" of American housing and banking disappeared some time ago.** Gone is the tightly regulated regime dominated by savings and loans connecting local borrowers and savers, reliant on the standard, thirty-year self-amortizing mortgage held on the lender's books; **we now have something much more spatially complex, dynamic, and risky**. (Wyly, et. al., 2012 – emphasis added)

That opening sentence is about as ethnocentric as a statement on housing and banking can get. Any time you see white people using the term "golden age" you know that they are referring to a period that ain't got no niggas in it. It's like

"Happy Days" and "Roaring '20s" – white heydays that festered in segregation and partied while black people lived "across the tracks" and "down by the levee."

And because of that reality, the next statement regarding the claim that "we now have something much more spatially complex, dynamic, and risky" is just as biased. Who is "we"? The world of housing that black people lived in was always "risky" and "complex." White people's problems are nothing like black people's problems, and therefore the housing concerns that face them, even the ones involving "space," are far different. It's difficult to have space issues when you live in a community where the population density is sky-high.

The lack of a job or high unemployment paved the way for many of the housing-related issues that black people faced:

> For most of the post-World War II period, American housing was a Keynesian arrangement, in which **the economics of supply-side housing construction cycles were governed by the "fundamentals" of demand for housing as a consumption good, paid for by the wages of an industrial economy.** But postindustrialism and deregulated financialization created a more unstable post-Keynesian network of supply-side profit opportunities that were partly unhinged from wages and other fundamentals. **Homes, borrowers, and financial obligations became the vehicles for capital accumulation backed by (and driven by) the steady rise in home prices** … (Wyly, et. al., 2012 – emphasis added)

Two key points are made once stripped of the poly-syllabic verbiage that these writers uses to talk over the head of readers. In that way you can claim to be exposing a wrong but you do it in such a way that the reader automatically assumes that you are an "expert" because of the words you use. But the fact is, "dress a liar as you will, a liar is a liar, still." Let's interpret the previous passage and how it actually relates to "race" and more specifically, to black people.

In the first instance, the talk of Keynesian fundamentals which basically means that people go to work, get paid and based on that group, housing is provided to meet the needs of those people. Housing becomes consumption good and the potential resident pays to a landlord who earns money which ploughs back into the economy and indirectly feeds back into the economic well-being of those providing the jobs.

This doesn't apply when the variable of "race" is applied. Housing is about providing where there is a need, but those needs have to be those of white folks. When it comes to black folks, the response is slum dwellings, public housing and enabling white homeowners to relocate, leave their housing behind, and then assist in cutting up those houses into smaller units (known as "rooms" or "flats") and that is how the housing needs of blacks are met. Even when the pay is almost the same, the variable of race determines the quality of the house and where the house will be located. This is known as "steering" and "redlining" and it is controlled by the bankers and other lending interests.

In the second instance, what is being said is that financial obligations of various kinds become the way to obtain and save money and therefore once the price of housing goes up, the area's population can adjust and meet the price that is being requested. Again, when you add the variable of "race," this equation becomes skewed. Because of the wage differential and the fact that blacks are charged more for even the lousy housing they have to live in, there is less disposable income that is in need of "adjusting." Not only that, but the housing prices rise based on location and quality and the system does not "allow" black people to have those types of options. Their "place" (literally and figuratively) is in that same area, so the main option for them is to build or modify where they live and be happy to have a place to live within the squalor of the ghetto universe.

> **Housing became a nexus between the slow materialities of place and the accelerating velocity of financial innovation and regulatory evasion.** Mortgage finance became a sector with its own partly autonomous dynamics of production, consumption, and speculation. (Wyly, et. al., 2012 – emphasis added)

But here's the difference: those "slow materialities of place" and the "accelerating velocity of financial innovation increasingly become a larger burden on black people. The white folks get raises, promotions and other financial opportunities that enable them to keep up with that financial innovation that banks claim to be engaged in. As those interests increase in cost, it becomes more difficult to meet the increase in meeting those costs – if you're black and poor, that is.

Then there is the variable of "regulatory evasion." That is what is rarely reported to the housing resident because the "financial innovation" is what is being promoted and paid for. Those "regulatory evasions" are the tactics used by the banks that merely pass any costs on to the consumer, perhaps wrapping it up on the "financial innovation package." One set of "offerings" for whites and those who live in favored zip codes, and another one for the low income and minority.

Skipping past the tendency to give credit to white economists, we will instead stick to the issues of housing, race and urban planning. The combination of these three elements, not necessarily in that order, continue to be the key and core of the black condition to this very day.

Historically speaking, for a moment, we find that,

> In the United States, the fundamental scale conflict in law and politics involves the state-federal tensions first negotiated through the Federalist Papers … **The state-federal axis has been remade slowly over time, with evolving geographies of urbanization, immigration, electoral competition, and the regional contours of racial and ethnic identity.** (Wyly, et. al., 2012 – emphasis added)

One of the thrusts of the Federalist Papers (which I read) was dealing with the "tyranny of the minority." The fear was that a few people would take over the country and then, in a somewhat authoritarian style, begin to impose rules and regulations on the masses. With that in mind the idea of "evolving geographies" takes on a different meaning, since "urbanization, immigration, electoral competition, and the regional contours of race and ethnic identity are all defined by a few in power and not only that, are RANKED according to need and utility.

In simple terms, electoral competition is a façade where two sides appear to be opposing each other but in reality they represent the same white supremacy vision and outcome – just like the Founding Fathers did. Urbanization is reserved for those who are "favored" while others are ruralized and placed on the urban fringe or some area near hazardous factories, warehouses or waterways. Immigration, even to this day in 2018, is feared because it will alter the racial character (read: lily-white) of America and what it TRULY stands for, and this defines the other areas and ensures that the "regional contours of racial and ethnic identity" remains segregated – from separate but equal to equal but separate.

Moving right along:

> The American racial state, therefore, can be understood as the sequence of legislative and judicial attempts to adapt and interpret a seventeenth-century document written by **slave-owning merchant classes yearning to be free**—to cope with the jurisdictional battles **as capital circulates more widely** and **encompasses growing shares of people and places once defined as racially and economically "marginal."** (Wyly, et. al., 2012 – emphasis added).

Three points will be made here in order to correct the previous statements that were just shared with you.

First, the very fact that the major documents of this country were put together by people who were slave holders should place the validity of those documents into serious question. People who own slaves are already engaging in what could be called "fragmentation of the human whole." They believe in a hierarchy of man, with those who are owned being under the control of those who are owners. This sets the stage for the racial and urban approaches, paradigms, projects and claims that are made thereafter. The fact was then, as it is now, quite simple: white people, in general, hate black people, in general. History bears this out quite emphatically.

Secondly, the belief that "capital circulates more widely", as if increasing numbers of people have access to it. In a commodity society there are those who have and those who don't have. Just because you get a nickel doesn't put you on the same level as someone with a hundred dollars and a farm. Capitalists can exist without having any capital – but they don't have any power or ability to expand their capital base. Capital may circulate, but it circulates in a way where the revenue streams all end up in the hands of the few. Karl Marx wrote long ago that, "The circulation of capital realizes value while living labor creates value." There is therefore a huge difference.

Third and finally, the claim that capital "encompasses growing shares of people and places once defined as racially and economically "marginal." Again, the assumption is that capital brings more people in and everybody benefits equally. Those who were enslaved were a part of the capitalist system and after being emancipated may have even considered themselves capitalists as they worked the fields while sharecropping. But just because they believe it doesn't make it so. Just because the pool expands doesn't mean that everyone in the pool benefits equally. Within that pool are the ones who work and the ones who control, with the latter group controlling almost all of the capital.

Because of the errors pointed out in the previous quote, distortions extend into other areas of analysis, such as the one that follows:

> For a short but important period in the twentieth century, these contradictions were partly resolved through the spatiality of the modern metropolitan welfare state—**symbolized by high-modernist, high-rise public housing at the core, and white middle-class owner-occupied housing on the expanding suburban fringe.** (Wyly, et. al., 2012)

What was just described is the sector model, where public housing was like a city unto itself surrounded by independent leeches with large houses and residents who generated capital and made decisions for the residents in that public housing. In other words, public housing resegregated people and made the residents totally dependent upon the system which, in turn, further enriched the system by creating a modern day "slave state" made up of the poor. Owner-occupied housing on the urban fringe was occupied by the cowards who packed up and ran when they saw black people entering the city. Those vacated lots were the places where the public housing was built to ensure that black migrants "stayed in and knew their 'place'."

To ensure that segregation paid off economically AND politically, there had to be the "master class" that called the shots and dictated the roles that the powerless would play:

> **The local white-ethnic political machines of northern industrial cities got federal help to rebuild their inner-city slums without disturbing established regimes of neighborhood segregation,** while the broad coalitions of national and regional conservatism reaped the rewards of racially exclusionary FHA mortgage insurance, tax subsidies for ownership, **and massive investments in the interstate highway system.** (Wyly, et. al., 2012 – emphasis added)

The previous quote contains two keys that ensured the on-going maintenance of external control of the land of the inner city, the housing that was located on that land, and the people who lived in that housing.

The first is the white political machine. Yes "machine."These cities had these white boys called "bosses" who ran the city like it was their own personal club. Among the more well-known were Boss Dahlman (Omaha), Pendergast (Kansas City), Crump (Memphis), Richard Daley (Chicago), and with the South being so backwards, the "bosses" there could control entire states, and they were Huey Long of Louisiana and Theodore Bilbo of Mississippi. And both states remain crime-ridden. Each of them had black flunkies who served as "overseers" and reported back to "the massa" to make sure that the white-run city (or state) remained under white domination.

The second key to ensuring maintenance of external control of the inner city and its residents was the use of interstates and freeways. The strategy was clear enough and began in the late 1940s:

> The urban planner Robert Moses was one of the first to propose the idea of using highways to "redeem" urban areas. In 1949, the commissioner of the Bureau of Public Roads, Thomas MacDonald, even tried to include the idea of highway construction as a technique for urban renewal in a national housing bill. (He was rebuffed.) But in cities across America, especially those that didn't want to—or couldn't—spend their own money for so-called urban renewal, the idea began to take hold. **They could have their highways and they could get rid of their slums. With just one surgery, they could put in more arteries, and they could remove the city's heart.** (Semuels, 2016 – emphasis added).

When the highways were built, supposedly to accommodate increasing numbers of cars, the white man made sure that they cleaved through black areas as much as possible. A large number of cities became disrupted and re-configured once decision makers ran freeways through them. At the top of my list are Omaha, Nebraska (I-75), Detroit (I-70), Oakland (I-980), Denver (I-70) and lest we forget the destruction of entire cities like Rondo, Minnesota.

With these two actions out of the way and established as permanent realities in the urban core (political control by the city administration and the interstate system), those in power could get on about the business of expanding into suburbia and after that, exurbia. Put another way,

> Ironically, the largest welfare program in American history—**the vast greenfield vistas of suburban houses for middle-class whites**—is **falsely remembered** as a golden age of the private market. By contrast, the most concentrated loci of affirmative efforts to help the racialized victims of housing market failure—federally funded, publicly owned housing—**were built only in those cities that actively sought the money, and only for a few years**. (Wyly, et. al., 2012 – emphasis added)

A few points should be made here.

To begin with, those suburban homes for middle-class America are not "false remembered." In fact they still exist. They are now inhabitated by those who once lived in the slums. Through ethnic succession, low income white folks inherited those early suburban homes while the former residents move on. The Jews begin the exodus and then come the Irish, the Italians and Germans, each one inheriting the housing left by the others. Remaining behind are the people with skin color, mainly Black and Brown folk. This reality is not "falsely remembered:' as long as it is remembered and is still being complied with, that is all that matters to the system and its form of racial and urban housing.

Another point is the claim that federal funding for public owned housing was built "only in those cities that sought the money and only for a few years." That is a half truth. The money was accepted based on promotions by the Feds akin to the "go west young man, go west" slogan. Free grant money to "develop the slums" was being given away to anyone who wanted it. You need not "actively seek" the money – just send in a short letter or a half-assed application and there was the check. All you had to prove was that your city had a "pocket of poverty" and a sizable number of black folk.

As for lasting on a few years, that is where the half-truth comes in. The "few years" is not accurate because those programs for public housing change and are modified over the years. So while "urban renewal" may peter out, it is replaced by "Model Cities" and then come the "Neighborhood Stabilization," "NeighborWORKS Homeownership," and the advent of Freddie Mac and Fannie Mae. They all got a lot. They might be short-lived, but right behind them came a new scam, a new target group (e.g., "black elderly," "black first-time homebuyers," "black veterans," etc.).

Everybody had a job, from top to bottom, when it came to the housing industry. An industry that wouldn't hire black people. The people being exploited were under-employed and many of the people in those communities couldn't even find work. More companies, more subsidiaries and more agencies popped up, meaning more jobs for white men. Furthermore,

> By the late 1990s the mortgage market was split across six regulatory agencies: the Office of the Comptroller of the Currency, the Federal Reserve Board, the Federal Deposit Insurance Corporation, the Office of Thrift Supervision, the National Credit Union Administration, and the U.S. Department of Housing and Urban Development. After the repeal of Depression-era banking laws with the Gramm-Leach-Bliley Act in 1998, the regulatory matrix become even more complex with large, multisubsidiary holding companies.[57] (Wyly, et. al., 2012)

Notice the high levels of organization and complexity that is involved when it comes to monitoring and collecting; how much organizational development is involved when it comes to overseeing and assessing. But these same white men, the master's of bureaucracy, cannot find it in their business plan to include treating people of color humanely and fairly. Their concept of "efficiency" is profit-driven, and this is the way it has been since the inception of the housing and banking systems.

Once the subprime "scam" went beyond the black community and into the areas where Latinos, Indians and low-income white folks were the dominant "targets" (it is being called the "sunbelt" in the Wyly article), politics became the name of the game and this created additional problems:

> Subprime expansion beyond the confines of northern inner cities into the expanding Sun Belt suburbs has devastated housing wealth—and all the conservative ideological promises of home ownership—in precisely those places where Democratic and Republican competition is most fierce, and where the coalition of economic and cultural conservatives is most unstable. This becomes clear from the foreclosure and delinquency estimates compiled as part of the Neighborhood Stabilization Program … (Wyly, et. al., 2012).

The areas hit were low-income whites, Latinos and working class black folks. Specifically,

> While many of the highest local delinquency rates appear in the safe
> Democratic seats of northern deindustrializing cities, the
> largest *number* of foreclosures hit hardest in a mixture of
> Democratic and Republican districts in the states that appear …
> **parts of North Las Vegas, Victorville, and other centers across
> Riverside and San Bernardino counties in California's Inland
> Empire, the Phoenix area, and Miami-Dade**. (Wyly, et. al., 2012
> – emphasis added)

Low income people being targeted by the powers that be. And that's the way race and housing have combined to define the standard of living in America ever since its inception. White folks are just now catching hell but even with them they can bail out with various forms of "white privilege." The more conservative the area, the more racist the policies, the more likely the banking industry was going to follow suit.

For instance,

> The single hardest-hit neighborhood in the nation, a block group
> with more than two thousand foreclosure starts as of May 2010, is in
> a patchwork of master-planned communities in the San Tan Valley
> in Arizona's Sixth Congressional District, southeast of Phoenix. This
> is Goldwater territory, about two-thirds Anglo white and one-quarter
> Latino, represented by the rock-solid conservative commitments of
> Jeff Flake. (Wyly, et. al. 2012).

Remember, the article being analyzed was published in 2012 – a half dozen years ago. Even though the area described was conservative, the President of the United States was not – it was Barack Obama. The banking scandals were being addressed and he bailed out those banks. But those banks turned around and did the same thing. But that notwithstanding, in today's America there is a madman who is not only racist and conservative, but also a member of the same billionaire class that benefited from the subprime scams in the first place. Flake has toned down his rhetoric but that's only because he's decided not to run for office again. Arizona remains conservative and racist and that means that black people, Latinos and First Nation people will continue to receive the short end of the stick.

Times do not look good:

> Flake's opposition to foreclosure relief—in early 2009, he tweeted,
> "my constituents wonder why they have to keep paying for others'
> mistakes"—nicely symbolizes the Right's attempts to restore the
> natural affinity of home ownership with the cult of John Galt heroic
> individual entrepreneurialism. The Right's coalition of cultural and
> economic conservatives seems to be holding for now. **But the**

> **alliance is unstable, and it is becoming harder to find scapegoats
> for the devastation of the home equity premiums once provided
> by suburban white privilege.** (Wyly, et. al., 2012 – emphasis
> added)

Flake was wrong. It is never hard to find scapegoats based on race. You may have to shift geographic positions and search other venues, but as long as you "target" the people with the skin color, the ones who are already being denied and degraded by the system, you have a ready-made pool of individuals who, despite having been raped by the banks, nevertheless continue to believe in "the American Dream." And the key to that dream, according to American mythology, is home ownership.

POLITICS OF RACE AND HOUSING, 2012

The history of race and housing set the stage for what we have today, and since the positions of the central characters (the "haves" versus the "have-nots") is essentially the same, the outcome is rigged by the haves so that the disparities and discrimination that have long permeated the housing scene when it comes to race continue on unabated.

Again, Wyly:

> Housing in America, once the foundation of a national identity of
> domestic family security and economic upward mobility, **is deeply
> unstable in today's rapidly shifting racial state.** Housing was at
> the birth of America's latest lurch to the right: Rick Santelli's call for
> "a tea party" went viral after the financial **anchor screamed about
> "bailing out the losers" when news broke in early 2009 that the
> Obama administration was considering plans to write down a
> small part of the principal for some mortgages.** (Wyly, et. al.,
> 2012 – emphasis added)

The "shifting racial state" must be another way of saying "from bad to worse." In either situation, whites make the money and black people continue to receive short shrift.

As for Obama "bailing out losers," he bailed out the banks and the real losers (the people left with the debt) were left to fend for themselves. Not only that but the "tea party's call" was not the reason for concerns about Obama's move; Obama was black and that kicked off all the pent-up hatred that these white people had long held for black people. The subprime controversy was just an avenue that they used to cover-up their centuries long ire.

If the source is racist in its purpose and outcomes, then modifications of that source will not solve the problem. Be that as it may, check out what Wyly writes in the following passage:

> The administration quickly backed off and **was able to get Congress** to agree to only very limited programs helping borrowers—most of them requiring the voluntary participation of mortgage servicers. We are now half a decade into the American Housing Depression. By the time the Republican primary contest heated up in early 2012, the American Right was working furiously to **restore the ideological stability of capital accumulation, consumer responsibility, and corporate rights.** (Wyly, et. al., 2012 emphasis added)

When you write the history of an issue, you have to approach it with as little bias as possible. Although it is impossible to be totally objective, you have to at least weigh both sides of an issue and not allow your ideological predispositions to get the best of you. Wyly falls short in the previous statement on at least two points.

First, merely skimming over the fact that "the administration … was able to get Congress to agree …" Just like that? How was this possible? It was possible because the administration and the Congress are both overwhelmingly white, and they saw the potential in an approach where cutting back on the number of "borrower help" programs could ameliorate some of the controversy. These agreements can be made when financial benefit for whites is the goal, but why couldn't that same administration and Congress get together and put an end to housing discrimination, redlining, steering and on-going gerrymandering?

Secondly, the claim that the "American Right" was working to "restore the ideological stability of capital accumulation, consumer responsibility, and corporate rights" is absurd. How can you restore what already existed? It's not like these elements disappeared from sight – they were just askew because, as usual, the white man dived in and tested the water with both feet and didn't account for certain social and economic factors. The national conflict exposed weaknesses in the program and those at the top and the conservatives tightened it up and modified things. See the difference?

Changes were made right away because they were needed in order to keep the revenue stream alive and to prevent social disruptions. Check it out:

> Gone was the "shocked disbelief " of a Fed chairman forced to admit in open congressional testimony that his "**whole intellectual edifice" had collapsed.** Once again, the national conversation went back to the Right's familiar Reagan mantra: government is not the

> solution to the problem, **government *is* the problem** … In the
> populist conservative imagination, it is all about public debt, and too
> much government spending going to help others—*those* people,
> everyone but me, us, and ours—**all those *others***. (Wyly, et. al., 2012
> – emphasis added)

This is what these power mongers do. When caught with their hands in the cookie jar, they do not condemn the system that they represent and are beholden to; they make it personal, as if they and they alone were the sole culprits. When the Fed chairman had the audacity to take the blame about his "whole intellectual edifice" had collapsed it was as if he was the brains behind the scam. The Fed chairman was just a lackey carrying out the program under the ideological watchful eye of his higher-ups. He took the blame because in white culture that is what they do – they call it "falling on their swords."

The idea that "government is the problem" is an abstractification. It's like saying invisible ghosts cause it to rain. Government is made up of white men who share in the ideology of white supremacy and then use racism and discrimination as its bulwark. But even in that these white men blame another set of white men as being "the government" (e.g., Republican vs. Democrat) so as not to indict the white supremacist structure.

And since that is the case, it is obvious and most evident who "all those others" are. When whites say "those people" they are talking about people who are different in color for the most part. And these are the people who are targeted when it comes to the modern day issue of race and housing.

As is the case with the conservative element (as if there's a difference), there is always one "coon" who is marched out to tow the white man's line or carry his water. Wyly singles out one Herman Cain, the former president of Godfather's Pizza and Republican presidential candidate:

> American capital achieves its fixes through a hybrid racial state. One
> part of the racial state is the fluid, dynamic interplay of images,
> discourses, and ideologies used to fight over the meanings of racial
> categories and their political mobilization … **Thus we have
> Herman Cain's meteoric trajectory as a one-hit-wonder
> Republican primary candidate achieving popularity with his "9-
> 9-9" tax plan that maps the way to the Steve Forbes flat-tax
> world**. (Wyly, et. al., 2012 – emphasis added).

The previous excerpt is why black people should study and write. Even whites who believe that they are being objective and "scientific" do not know about the black experience. Herman Cain is what most black people would call an "uncle tom" and he as much as admits it. He has nothing to do with the black community or giving back to the neighborhoods but because he has black skin he is deemed a black leader by white outsiders who pay homage to the fact that he is wealthy.

Using that as our criteria, there was nothing "meteoric" about his "trajectory" in the Republican Party or as a primary candidate. He was a joke, a token that was used so that the lily-whiteness of the long list of Republican presidential candidates would be able to hide its lily-whiteness. He knew what he was and he knew he was outmatched. Most of the "coons" of his ilk enter these contests (i.e., Lenora Fulani, Jesse Jackson) so that they can garner black confidence and a few votes and then, once they inevitably get eliminated from the pack, they sign their voters over to the white man who offers them the most money.

That "9-9-9" tax plan that Cain put forth was a joke. It should have been called the "nein-nein-nein" plan, since "nein" is German for "no." The world that Cain was catering to was a world that most blacks do not understand and have not entered into. And with all that money he – like so many black and Latino leaders before him – was brought down due to some ghetto shit. Wyly writes,

> **When sexual harassment allegations sent Cain's campaign into a nosedive, Cain joked that he wondered if Anita Hill might not endorse him**. A few months later he appeared on Bill Maher's "Real Time" in front of a poster advertising the "documentary" film *Runaway Slave: From Tyranny to Liberty. Runaway Slave* **"discovers the unknown history of the Civil Rights Movement"** and "exposes the NAACP as a mouthpiece of the Democratic Party, and the NAACP's leaders as the **ultimate 'race hustlers' who perpetuate—and profit—from a victim mentality that hurts the African-American community"** …(Wyly, et. al., 2012 –e mphasis added).

The truth can be spoken even amidst jest, hyperbole and grandiose statements that often contradict the way that we have been programmed to think about and see things. The previous passage proves this to be the case on three levels.

First, to use Anita Hill's previous situation as the butt of a joke to bail himself out goes directly to the character of this asshole. In vintage "conservative" fashion, these men think they can say and do anything and get away with it. Anita Hill was victimized by a negro the same color as Cain and sharing a similar class standing. Clarence Thomas got away with it because he did the same thing Cain just did to Ms. Hill: Cain used her case to make it appear as if he was really 'grass roots' and had 'street cred,' and Thomas did the same thing during his hearing when he uttered the term "high-tech lynching."

The second level of race-related error lies in the claim that the history of the civil rights movement could be "discovered." Even before knowing anything about the movie the claim that a movie can "discover" something about a black movement tells you that it will be filled with error. For instance, black people were not "slaves," but prisoners of war. A slave does not wish to escape because the "master" has control of his mind. LaRue Nedd spells this out in his book *Why We Shouldn't Call Our Foreparents Slaves.* And the title: how can you run from slavery to "liberty" when liberty is a state of "freedom from" something. Black people are not free, and you need only glean the information on racial disparities to see that this is the case.

Appearing on the Bill Maher show, knowing what we know now, is quite appropriate. This white man, Maher, donated a million dollars to the Obama campaign and is known as what we would call a white "liberal." He think that he's down with the 'hood and all that bullshit. Karenga (1967) once wrote that, "A racist is like a dog; you can teach it to stand on its hind legs (being liberal), but it eventually falls back to all fours." Maher got so comfortable that during an episode of his weekly HBO show, "Real Time," on or about June 3rd, Mayer was interviewing Ben Sasse, a hick senator from Nebraska, and when Sasse said something about coming out to the (corn) fields and work with us, Maher said: "Work in the fields? Senator, I'm a house nigger. No, it's a joke."

This is of course in reference to Malcolm X's speech distinguishing between the field "NEGRO" and the house "NEGRO." But the point to be made is that Ice Cube came on and explained to Maher about becoming "too familiar" with white people. Once black people do that, whites feel they can say anything around those blacks. That is not the case.

When you have liberty you are trying to get away from something. That is not what black people appear to be doing. They are striving to become a part of a system that hates their guts. Most people refer to it as "integration" or "inclusion." The history of the civil rights movement is a movement that was largely co-opted by white people like Rockefeller, who paid $800,000 to six civil rights leaders to "take over" the movement and he (Rockefeller) and his fellow whites would give them all the media attention (plus the money to divide) that they needed.

Who were these negroes, known as "The Big Six"? They were Martin Luther King, the NAACP's Roy Wilkins, the Urban League's Whitney Young, John Lewis of the Student National Coordinating Committee (SNCC), James Farmer of the Congress of Racial Equality (CORE) and A Philip Randolph a black union leader. Civil rights cannot be "given" – they can only be exercised. But when you use the term civil rights, just like when Clarence Thomas used "high tech lynching," you can get the white man's attention.

The third element lies in Cain's description of the NAACP (by way of the "documentary" poster) depicting the NAACP's leaders as the ultimate 'race hustlers' who perpetuate—and profit—from a victim mentality that hurts the African-American community". This goes back to the title of the movie. How can you talk about liberty, implying "freedom from," when you are running back to your master begging him for inclusion and acceptance. In other words what Cain was saying about the NAACP is true: they shake down white people for discriminating against black people and they get paid to go away while the discrimination continues.

So to single out Cain, even in an article about banking and his corporate values, is a choice that the authors of the article made. The background information I have just provided you with was omitted in the same way that black-oriented facts are omitted from the planners, developers, contractors and city officials who are busy day and night dominating and directing the lives of black people.

People like Cain and articles like the one by Wyly are focused on showing that there has been "progress" in race relations and in this particular case, in housing for people of color. For instance, Wyly writes the following about the documentary mentioned earlier:

> Produced by Dick Armey's FreedomWorks, *RunawaySlave* declares that "while the African-American community **has triumphed over the scourge of physical slavery,** many still suffer from a mental slavery—to government" … (Wyly, et. al., 2012 – emphasis added)

In America whites and blacks are still victims of "wage slavery." Just because a person gets paid doesn't mean that they don't have the mentality of slaves. Blacks were not slaves back during the antebellum days because on numerous levels we resisted. But today, the slave exists: people with options that they will not consider out of fear for losing their jobs. Now THAT is the thinking of a slave. And the "mental slavery" is not just to the government because the government is a white institution and institutions are designed to perpetuate entire systems. And the system in question is the same one that Wyly is writing for and had her publication approved by: the system of white supremacy.

The "politics of race and housing" in present-day America shows that those in control and those who do the talking and promoting are still confused. And in that confusion they tend to confuse those who look to them for information and assistance. As long as the mythology continues, the problems will persist. Not only the problems of housing discrimination, subprime lending and outright racial and residential segregation, but the problems that perpetuate poverty which, in turn, negative impacts on black lives and the quality of life.

Note, for instance, the following excerpt from the Wyly piece:

> **Anita Hill is right that "the American Dream means nothing if it is not inclusive,"** but so is Derrick Bell when he demands that we "'Get Real' about race and racism in America" … **One part of getting real involves building the infrastructure of discrimination enforcement that was stripped out of civil rights legislation in the 1960s and 1970s to avoid Southern filibusters** … That might offer a first step toward the "simplified and clarified" meaning of housing in America, **"with a renewed emphasis on shelter and neighborhood" as well as genuine equality …** (Wyly, et. al., 2012 – emphasis added)

Three points of correction are in order before moving on to the next section of this book.

To begin with there is no "American Dream" that is all-inclusive. When white people coined that moniker in 1931. As one source explains,

> The American Dream is a national ethos of the United States, the set of ideals (democracy, rights, liberty, opportunity and equality) in which freedom includes the opportunity for prosperity and success, as well as an upward social mobility for the family and children, achieved through hard work in a society with few barriers. In the definition of the American Dream by James Truslow Adams in 1931, "life should be better and richer and fuller for everyone, with opportunity for each according to ability or achievement" regardless of social class or circumstances of birth. (Wikipedia, 2018)

It should be clear that whites were speaking of themselves and not First Nation, African Americans or Latinos. This is proven through their own actions including the subject of this book, land use and housing manipulation.

Secondly, regarding the "building of an infrastructure of discrimination enforcement." What is meant is probably "anti-discrimination enforcement" but in either case it's a fantasy. Discrimination is based on preference and white folks prefer their own people over all others, qualified or not, deserving or not. And filibusters are not just "Southern" in their basis or application; for example, white folks have been "filibustering" against human rights for blacks, especially in fair housing, for more than two centuries.

Third, the statement regarding, "a renewed emphasis on shelter and neighborhood as well as genuine equality." How can something be "renewed" when it never existed in the first place?

THE GHETTO AND PREDATORY LENDING

The black community has been a "target" of America's pollution ever since their arrival in the North after migrating from the Deep South in the 1800s. I liken it to various forms of pollution and better yet, as a socioeconomic form of "toxic racism."

The term "toxic racism" was coined to describe this long-term tradition and tendency. Marvin Gaye's "What's Goin' On" is used as a source to show that such pollution is no fluke. An article in the February 28, 2018 edition of *The Atlantic* further explains,

> Gaye's prophecies relied on the qualitative data of storytelling—of long-circulated anecdotes and warnings within black communities of bad air and water, poison, and cancer. But those warnings have been buttressed by **study after study indicating that people of color face disproportionate risks from pollution,** and that polluting industries are often located in the middle of their communities. (Newkirk, 2018 – emphasis added)

In light of this reality, I view predatory lending as being akin to toxic racism. It is pervasive, it is targeted and it can "poison" the lives of people of color in both the short- and long-term. This section will clearly establish the toxicity of predatory lending and its impact on black and minority communities.

Wyly asserts the following:

> **Between 2004 and 2010 the market share of high-risk subprime mortgages to single black women was almost four times the share for Anglo white couples**. But Wall Street sees a different view: Anglo white couples outnumber single black women three to one. Wall Street made it clear that local brokers and lenders could target any submarket, any community that made sense in a particular urban and regional context—**so long as borrowers were delivered to feed the vast securitization machine** (Wyly, et. al., 2012 – emphasis added)

Those in power will do anything to exploit race, but when it is clear that they are racists, they want to use their numbers to make their tactics appear otherwise. So what if white couples outnumber single black women three to one, and so what if they are also vulnerable to exploitation: the white Anglo couple is white in a society where whiteness is valued above all else. Do you honestly think that the white decision maker is going to treat his own race members the same as he does a person of color, deemed historically as the bane of his existence? Of course not. There are poor white people, make no doubt about it; but they ain't po' because they're white!

> **This simulacra racial state moves fast: racial images, categories, and politics move like mercury.** It does have serious performative consequences, and thus **the critical Left must always be in the arena to challenge the evasive new constructions of white privilege manufactured by the powerful coalitions of capital and racism.** But another part of the project must devote attention to the old-fashioned material inequalities that are still quite literally *located* in real places and real neighborhoods. This part of the American racial state involves the layering of fast capital on a mixture of urban landscapes—**some of them rapidly growing, others quickly declining, others slow and stable.** (Wyly, et. al., 2012 – emphasis added)

Correction is in order as it related to the previous excerpt.

First off, the term "simulacra" is not accurate because it means an imitation of a person or thing – in this case, the racial state. The racial state, including those images, categories and politics that Wyly claims "move like mercury" do not move like that. Racism and all of its mechanisms move slowly and steadily. Discrimination may move quickly, but it is only an offshoot or manifestation of the pervasive racist umbrella. Wyly needs to get it straight because ignorance of racism clouds much of what is being written about housing and its history.

Secondly, since when has "the Left" challenged white privilege and/or capitalistic-based racism? The Left is a key cog in it! It is the so-called left (the sons and daughters of the racist right) that provides the smokescreen necessary to dupe society into believing that America is not the capitalist contraption that it has historically been. The Left is key: held up as examples are Abraham Lincoln, Gloria Steinem, John Brown and many of the civil rights and black power advocates. But what do every single one of them share in common? With all their talk and grandiose rhetoric, every single one of them continues to promote "integration" as the key vision and goal. And with integration being promoted, the capitalist racist system grows exponentially. The Left is nothing more than a group of water carriers and lackeys for the Right.

Third, the talk about urban landscapes and how "some of them rapidly growing, others quickly declining, others slow and stable." More bullshit.

The urban landscape is black and generally non-white. According to the U.S. Census, "About 6 in 10 people reporting as Black or African American, alone or in combination with other races, resided in 10 states where nearly half the U.S. population lived last year, according to new Census 2000 analysis released today by the Commerce Department's Census Bureau" (United States Census, 2010). That was eight years ago and we know it's grown darker since, with the influx or more immigrants of color headed into the ghetto to partake in their contribution to "ethnic succession."

Furthermore, according to the International Business Times,

> Minorities outnumber non-Hispanic whites in nearly a quarter of America's largest urban areas, a demographic development that is likely to **expand as booming minority populations outpace the country's static white populations**. (White, 2011 – emphasis added).

The only element that is "rapidly growing" is the black population. And that is being directed and funneled into the same ghettos that always existed. And it's not just black folks, either:

> Non-Hispanic whites are now **minority in 22 of the country's 100-biggest urban areas,** including those surrounding Washington, New York, San Diego, Las Vegas and Memphis. The reversal is being fueled by a **growth in Hispanic and Asian populations -- they grew by 41 and 43 percent, respectively** -- and the fact that white populations have grown by less than one percent. (White, 2011 – emphasis added) .

There you have it. Asians and Latinos are expanding and the white population is moving to the country or into the suburbs. The saying teaches that "as things change, so they remain the same."

More from Wyly and the racial history of housing:

> **The interplay of suburbanization, history, demography, and all the hidden biases of market practices and public policy help reinforce many of the old inequalities**. The evidence from the foreclosure disaster tells a painfully familiar story: using the most widespread ways of measuring segregation in the nation's one hundred largest metropolitan areas, J. S. Rugh and D. S. Massey find that **black-white residential segregation has a significant, independent effect on foreclosure** … (Wyly, et. al. 2012 – emphasis added).

What you just read is academic/intellectual bullshit. It's all about race. Suburbanization is about race (white folks running from black folks), history is all about race (enslavement of Africans brought to American shores, murder of First Nation people), demography is about race (the study to deal with the white man's fear of the "browning" of America) and so on. If you understand that, then you wouldn't be making reference to "the old inequalities." The inequalities from days of yore, going back to Europe and the American colonies, set the standards and serve as the models for the inequalities of today!

In light of the facts I have just laid before you, how can Wyly have the gall to make the claim that, "black-white residential segregation has a significant, independent effect on foreclosures." That is because white racism is the dominant ideology and housing discrimination is the umbrella that dominates land use decisions. Can it be made any more plain than that?

URBAN MODELS AS A BASIS FOR BLACK POLITICAL ACTION AND LEADERSHIP: A THEORY AND PROSPECTIVE PARADIGMS USING URBAN PLANNING MODELS

INTRODUCTION

> Production is not the application of tools to materials, but logic to work.
>
> ■ Peter F. Drucker

This book advances a new, supplemental approach to urban planning which I have named the Africentric Sociourban Planning paradigm. I am concerned about the fact that black people will always be an "urban" people, a decision made by the powers that be as they continue to load up the cities with those who are not white while the Caucasians skate toward the suburbs and exurbs. With this in mind there is a need for a discussion of the existing black urban planning models and how they can be modified to accommodate the future needs of these African-American (and Latino) enclaves as they are configured based on both class and race.

What I am about to describe is more "sociourban" than technical because African-Americans are a social people. As I quote elsewhere from a movie on the martial arts, "Technique is a trap, style is a prison – unless he is willing to be reborn." The same can be true about urban planning and its emphasis on form over function. This section of the book seeks to address both with more emphasis on the product of both, the long-term well-being of the people.

Why the Urban Models of Black Leadership?

In reality, when it comes to political development for African-American communities, there is no real "black leadership." There are black people who get elected to office and go through the motions, usually rubber stamping what white leadership says and then, since their constituents are as clueless as they are, continue to get elected back in to office time and time again, whether they are doing the work of the community or not. And so it has gone in all leadership areas, including urban planning leadership or, should I say, the dearth of it.

As Karenga (1967) wrote many years ago, "you cannot have political freedom without an economic base." Even leaders in the urban planning area know this to be the case because planning, in America, is political. And in being political, it is also racial. As it is in other spheres, the golden rule truly exists: "the man with the gold makes the rules. Put another way:

> If community building is to be effective, funders must carefully research their sites of intervention, and then wholeheartedly commit to the process, knowing that setbacks and frustrations will inevitably occur along the way. In addition, a realistic accounting needs to be openly undertaken of the multiple and dissimilar goals of stakeholders hoping to build neighborhood-based community. Poverty amelioration and preparing a neighborhood for capitalist investment can be antithetical agendas, reflected in dysjunctures between the ways that residents define the situation and the understandings that are adopted in city halls and foundations (Levy, 2000: p. 33).

What you just read above could be appropriately defined as "urban planning bullshit." Let me break it down for you concept-by-concept before we move on.

Sites of intervention? These people know where the low-income and minorities are to be found – they are the areas that these people work so hard to AVOID! That is, until there is a grant to be secured; if that is the case then "community-building" comes to mind almost immediately (as long as the white man/white organization is in charge). What makes them finally decide to "intervene"? Only when a crisis that might overflow the ghetto or barrio boundaries and head into suburbia where THEY live. Then, and only then, is it time for "something to be done."

An accounting of goals from among the stakeholders is not going to happen. The people with the money and the resources are going to set the standards and then assess who they want to bring along on any project or endeavor. The goals are to do something that is going to generate profit and/or pay for itself. The people in an area are secondary because the only reason they count to the stakeholders is because their social problems generate the basis for future grants and other revenue streams! If the stakeholders can't get paid, then for the most part they are not even interested!

Levy writes that, "Poverty amelioration and preparing a neighborhood for capitalist investment can be antithetical agendas …" Can be? They ARE! Furthermore the idea of "poverty amelioration" is not what capitalists want unless it is a matter of "ground clearing" or "smash and burn" where they are clearing the way for some major development. Poverty amelioration would wipe out the demographics needed to generate more free money from the federal and state agovernment. Poverty amelioration would mean no more Community Development Block Grant, no more Urban Development Block Grant, no more Community Service Block Grant, no more Weed and Seed and so on.

For these reasons there needs to be some black-oriented, black-directed and black-created Urban Planning Models done for us and by us. These are akin to the Africentric Sociourban Planning paradigm that I propose herein. Following however, are some subsets of my important concept.

Since the death of Martin Luther King, Jr., black leadership has, for the most part, been a major disappointment. Some would say that they have been an abysmal failure. They have become to system-oriented, too self-absorbed, too greedy, to obsessed with getting on television or getting their name in the papers, and generally naïve of the issues other than those they glean or gather from the easily assembled facts of the oppressor.

This indictment fits nearly all of them, from religious and civic leaders to political leaders and, in many cases, even the grass roots organizer types. Why these proposed urban models of black leadership? Simply, somebody has to do something. Some kind of standards have to be established so that, at very least, we will be able to see where these people are going, why they choose to lead, how they endeared themselves to the community, how they actually feel about black people (other than their friends and family members) and so on.

At present it seems that anyone can become a leader without actually having to be one. I've seen actual nitwits rise to the level of community wide observance in cities like Dallas, Milwaukee, and Omaha. And I've studied black leadership and their ideas and movements from the days of antebellum slavery up to the present. As a Black Studies scholar and instructor, I make it a point to know more about my history than any white man. As a result, I care more than most people because I've devoted myself to working toward digging us out of this rut that we've gotten ourselves in, mainly because of our police-dog like commitment to the concept of "integration."

Urban Models of Black Leadership, as described herein, borrowing from three models of urban land use, may sound grandiose. But at least it gives us a starting point, especially since black people seem to hell-bent on following anybody any place out of some misplaced sense of racial loyalty of "patriotism". That approach worked back in the day when our leadership was accountable to us; that is no longer the case. They now pay homage to white people, money, being on the down-low, white bitches, crack cocaine and a host of other secondary issues that take precedence over the long-term well-being of black folks.

Next, a synopsis and overview of the three urban land use models that I propose.

The Three Models of Urban Land/Leadership: Explanation

As an Urban Studies/Urban Planning student (graduate school at the University of Nebraska Omaha and the University of Iowa) I enjoyed this field of study immensely. I learned a great deal about zoning, urban law and legislation, public economy, utilities and how they are determined, construction of streets, tax incremental financing and so much more. As one interview regarding the study of land use informs us:

> The study of urban land use generally draws from three different descriptive models. These models were developed to generalize about the patterns of urban land use found in early industrial cities of the U.S. Because the shape and form of American cities changed over time, new models of urban land were developed to describe an urban landscape that was becoming increasingly complex and differentiated. (Levy, 2000: p. 33).

The models are important but they are mostly geographical and deal with land usage, shape and form. They are devoid of how those in charge manipulate these land forms and based upon what those in power deem as being "important," manipulate certain populations into different areas of these land forms for the sake of social control.

In previous sections of this book, I have shown how racial matters are hidden from the powers that be and how their orientation is on separating the races and making sure that people of color receive short shrift at every opportunity. With this as the ideological lynchpin that promotes white supremacy, it becomes clear that urban planning paradigms, on various levels, deal strictly with boundaries, structure and format and very little with human beings and issues of stratification, race and discrimination.

It should be noted that these models served as a basis for analysis, and were developed at different times. When placed together, they give urban planners a better understanding of city configurations, which translates to mean better ways to exploit them so that racial and class segregation is maintained. They are necessary in order to maintain the system, but when it comes to black people, the traditional models may not be sufficient. The fact is, nothing is perfect, and,

> … because these are general models devised to understand the overall patterns of land use, none of them can accurately describe patterns of

urban land use in all cities. In fact, all of these models have been criticized for being more applicable to cities in the U.S. than to cities of other nations. Other criticisms have focused on the fact that the models are static; they describe patterns of urban land use in a generic city, but do not describe the process by which land use changes.

And there is a reason why the processes that change the land use are not mentioned in the urban planning literature. It's because it is in the manipulation of those land uses that racism, discrimination and other types of man-made inequalities come into play. Just as the cities are shaped by certain geographical realities and needs-based applications, so too are the neighborhoods that make up these communities: segregation means that blacks will live in certain places, usually close to the water (known as "the bottoms") and whites will have free access to all else.

This is why black models or black-oriented models are needed.

As is the case in most instances where this society was in need of change, black people have to intervene and make sure that this society will develop something that includes "humanity." When this country was legally segregated, it was black people who had to march and fight and burn in order to change it. When the cops were getting away with murdering black men in the streets, black people – from the Black Panther Party for Self-Defense to Colin Kaepernick - had to bring attention to it. When the courts were giving black people time like it was lunch, we had to revolt and tell them that enough is enough, spearheaded by the incredible book by Michelle Alexander (*The New Jim Crow: Mass Incarceration in the Age of Color Blindness*).

And when it came to issues of land use, we should be doing the same thing, because an alien race is working day and night to determine what kind of "space" we (as blacks) will occupy. From the shack out back during enslavement to the northern slums following black migration, to modern-day ghettos, the urban planners and policymakers, developers and contractors, all work in unison to keep black folks at arm's length. The only way to deal with that is to develop model plans that are hacked out in our own image and interests.

Put another way, and serving as a necessary segue into what I am writing about, please note that,

> Despite these criticisms, these models continue to be useful generalizations of the way in which land is devoted to different uses within the city. Below, we will examine the Concentric Zone Model, Sector Model and Multiple Nuclei Model of urban land use. (Levy, 2000: p. 33).

Criticism only serves to make future ideas stronger. This is why I believe that these three models serve as a necessary foundation for the development of what I call generically call "Community Leadership Paradigms" and, more specifically, Urban Models of Black Leadership. Here is why.

To begin with, these models will enable us to establish patterns on the part of those black leaders and those who aspire to lead. These patterns will provide far more stability than anything we have now because for the most part, black people simply refuse to judge or critique black leadership. In recent years, this has served to hurt us, since those who think that they have carte blanche have opted to ignore their constituencies and opt, instead, to carve their own personal niches in the system or seek out riches (or sexual gratification) in some other capacity.

Secondly, like the urban land models, the models of black leadership are more applicable to cities and towns in the U.S. than in other nations. This is not to imply that black leadership throughout the Diaspora cannot be bought off or controlled by outside interests. But the black leadership models that I offer here speak to the unique contradiction that their constituents as well as the majority of people in this country seem to buy into: that being that in America, anyone can "make it," we're all equal, and that all of us have opportunities.

These lies, when placed in a real world context, point to many of the problems that black people face: we tend to believe in slogans, phrases, axioms, maxims and catch phrases even when we see the reality right in our face. This is how black leaders can get away with almost anything and yet continue to have large followings, constituencies, congregations and supporters.

Third, like the land use models, these black leaders are a static essence: they seem to act in the same way and there is no process by which their leadership changes or adapts to the needs of the people that they are leading. Almost all of them have Type A personalities and seem to bring with them a "my way or the highway" approach to leadership and community organizing. My models take this into account and do offer some suggestions that offer the masses of black people better options and alternatives when it comes to leadership selection.

Fourth, like the land use/leadership models – the ones I offer - hopefully offer "useful generalizations" of ways in which black leadership assumes and claims to be, as well as what it actually is, when it comes to the defense and development of their followers/constituents/congregants.

In the following section we will examine the Concentric Zone models , Sector Model, and Multiple Nuclei Model and of urban land use where each will be immediately followed up with my definitions of Urban Community Leadership. Once you get an overview of what these three models are about, then it will easier to understand the leadership styles that I developed based upon the previously described land use urban planning paradigm.

The Three Models of Urban Land Use/Community Leadership

The first land use form is called the "concentric zone model." This will be explained and then my concept of The Concentric Zone Model Community Leadership Paradigm will be defined and elaborated upon.

<u>Land Use: Concentric Zone</u>

Envision with me, if you will, a target, with the bull's eye in the middle and rings, white and black, surrounding that bull's eye. This is what the concentric zone model looks like: a central business district in the middle and then a ring around it consisting of neighborhoods, a ring around that consisting of services and then the outer rings, consisting of the suburbs and exurbs.

The concentric zone model, what we were taught is also known as the "Burgess Model," was supposedly created by sociologist Ernest Burgess in 1925.

Specifically, our textbooks inform us that Burgess identified five rings of land use that would form around the CBD. These rings were originally defined as the (1) central business district, (2) zone of transition, (3) zone of independent workers' homes, (4) zone of better residences and (5) zone of commuters. An important feature of this model is the positive correlation of socio-economic statuts of households with distance from the CBD -- more affluent households were observed to live at greater distances from the central city. The model was based on Burgess's observations of Chicago during the early years of the 20th century. Major routes of transportation emanated from the city's core, making the CBD the most accessible location in the city.

When it comes to Omaha, the concentric model once applied. Surrounding the downtown were the low income areas of the south side (Latino) and the North side (Black). But in recent years white folks have made the decision to "return" from those "outer ring" suburbs and exurbs because of the development of the river front which is contiguous to the downtown night life. As a result, the north Omaha black community is being systematically relocated to the northwest making room for whites to return to the inner city that they abandoned via "white flight" in the 1960s.

The Concentric Zone Community Leadership Paradigm

This is the model that describes Omaha more accurately out of the three in terms of geo-spatial arrangement. It is also the model that offers the potential to be the most far-reaching in terms of political and socioeconomic scope as it relates to the other populations across the city and even the state. However, as a leadership paradigm, I designed something that has never been considered, but if it was, the black community of North Omaha (conceptualized here as our "central business district") would have optimal and far-reaching leadership that would be diverse socioeconomically, but unified in terms of the collective agreement that North Omaha has to be the focus and fulcrum of attention, resource development and real empowerment.

And this same black leadership, most of whom are on the government dole in some capacity, would do anything to reject the idea lest their "master" become angered and the crumbs that they are allowed to scrounge for from the table of oppression become dried up.

Two representatives from the four outer rings would be a part of the **Concentric Council of Elders**, a total of eleven representatives (including three from the CBD) that would serve as the guiding/governmental body of the Concentric Zone Community Leadership Paradigm.

With North Omaha as our CBD (central "leadership" district), what each ring surrounding the area would represent would be supportive networks functioning, generally, in leadership specific capacities that, in turn, feed into the CBD thereby empowering and strengthening North Omaha (the CBD).

Directly surrounding and contiguous to the CBD is our **zone of transition**, an area where young leaders that we would be mentored – an area of protégés, close enough to the CBD but serving as a *"learning layer"* that would also be able to deal with the more stable leadership in the next sector. Two leaders from this area sit on the Concentric Council of Elders that serves as the governing body of the centrally located CBD. Mentored by all of the other zones, including the CBD, this is the zone that represents the future leaders of the paradigm.

In other words, this zone of transition would be responsible for learning all they could from the CBD, but also circulating and disseminating information about history, culture, economics, law and other areas, not only within their zone of transition, but also to the third ring of leaders, known herein as "the zone of independent thinkers' homes."

The **zone of independent thinkers** is made up of the intelligentsia, the brain trust for the community. Two leaders from this area sit on the Concentric Council of Elders that serves as the governing body of the centrally located CBD. The zone of independent thinkers is just that: working in the traditional system outside of the community but committing itself to work toward development of the CBD, while also mentoring the protégés from the "learning layer" previously decribed (zone of transition).

In addition to the zone of transition and the zone of independent thinker's homes, we have the **zone of logistics**. Two leaders from this area sit on the

Concentric Council of Elders that serves as the governing body of the centrally located CBD.

The zone of logistics is where the well-to-do members of the black community live, meaning that they have the financial wherewithal to host important meetings and fundraisers to finance the projects aimed at improving the CBD. These are the economic entities that plough monies into whatever is needed by the protégés, the independent workers and, of course, the CBD proper. That is why they are "independent"; they may work in the system but they don't necessarily have to. Because of their financial status, they might be corporate directors or living on an inheritance; at any rate, their location and status serve as a buffer against incursions from the majority community (both financially and physically) and again, they don't have to worry about "retaliation" from an employer or harassment by police because they are system-oriented "negroes" who have the best interests of the CBD and its residents at heart.

Finally is the **mobility zone** (known in urban planning as the zone of commuters). These would be the individuals who would be in charge of "diaspora relations," meaning that black people, no matter where they lived in Nebraska, would be recruited and incorporated into the expansion and beautification of the CBD (North Omaha). Two leaders from this area sit on the Concentric Council of Elders that serves as the governing body of the centrally located CBD. This is the zone where people live who are retired or independently wealthy, many hailing from and regularly interacting with the residents of the zone of logistics.

To recap: we have North Omaha as the central business district; then there is the zone of transition on the inner ring contiguous to the CBD, the zone of independent thinkers, the zone of logistics and finally, on the outer ring, the mobility zone. This is a proposal that can empower black folks who, at present, are powerless in a city where power is valued above all else.

Land Use: Sector Model

Sector model is when the city is cut into different "sections" and the central business district is located somewhere in the middle. Soon after Burgess generalized about the concentric zone form of the city, Homer Hoyt re-cast the concentric ring model. According to the research, while recognizing the value of the concentric ring model, Hoyt also observed some consistent patterns in many American cities. He observed, for example, that it was common for low-income households to be found in close proximity to railroad lines, and commercial establishments to be found along business thoroughfares. In 1939, Hoyt modified the concentric zone model to account for major transportation routes. (Beauregard, 2007).

Recall that most major cities evolved around the nexus of several important transport facilities such as railroads, sea ports, and trolly lines that eminated from the city's center. Recognizing that these routes (and later metropolitan expressways and interstate highways) represented lines of greater access, Hoyt theorized that cities would tend to grow in wedge-shaped patterns, or sectors, eminating from the CBD and centered on major transportation routes. Higher levels of access translate to higher land values. Thus, many commercial functions would remain in the CBD, but manufcaturing activity would develop in a wedge surrounding transport routes. (Wikipedia, 2018).

<u>The Sector Model Community Leadership Paradigm</u>

He observed, for example, that it was common for low-income households to be found in close proximity to railroad lines, and commercial establishments to be found along business thoroughfares. In 1939, Hoyt modified the concentric zone model to account for major transportation routes. Hoyt theorized that cities would tend to grow in wedge-shaped patterns, or sectors, eminating from the CBD and centered on major transportation routes. Higher levels of access translate to higher land values. Thus, many commercial functions would remain in the CBD, but manufacturing activity would develop in a wedge surrounding transport routes.

New Kemet Planning Bureau

Seeing this, I began to use my radio show and the Courier to shift into a brand new gear: noticing the segregation which permeated Milwaukee, I decided to address the segregation with a call for a new community. I decided, in 1989-90 to call it "New Kemet." Kmet is what Egypt was called before the name change, and it translates to mean "land of the blacks." Because of residential and racial segregation in Milwaukee, that is what the central city was – the land of the blacks. I sat down and wrote up by-laws, a constitution, and even an entire "city charter," using the city of Omaha's city charter as a format. I then worked out a preamble which went like this:

> WE, THE PEOPLE, citizens of Milwaukee and residents of the inner city, In order to form a more symbiotic set of relations, increase the prospects for mutual benefit, ensure internal stability, increase the area's tranquility, provide for common defense and development, promote the general welfare of each other, and secure the blessings of liberation to ourselves and our Posterity, do ordain and seek to establish, maintain and enhance the existence of the area of Omaha known hereafter as NEW KEMET.

This new community would have been the embodiment of the Africentric Sociourban Planning paradigm. The key, as I outlined it, was to intercept that community development money that was being abused by white city administrators under the false claim of "saving the black community" – which is what the money was earmarked for.

Recall that the Sector model is when the city is cut into different "sections" and the central business district is located somewhere in the middle. New Kemet was smack dab in the heart of the city of Milwaukee, not on the urban fringe. It would have been perfect for the ASP paradigm because it had its own gas stations, markets, super markets, several hospitals and the largest school in the nation, Milwaukee Area Technical College. If only I had more time …

Land Use: Multiple Nuclei

The third and final land use form is called the "multiple nuclei model." This will be explained and then the concept of The Multiple Nuclei Community Leadership Paradigm will be defined and elaborated upon.

In the multiple nuclei model, the city consists of several different areas and as such, there may be more than one business district to serve these various areas. By 1945, it was clear to Chauncy Harris and Edward Ullman that many cities did not fit the traditional concentric zone or sector model. Cities of greater size were developing substantial suburban areas and some suburbs, having reached significant size, were functioning like smaller busniess districts. These smaller business districts acted as satellite nodes, or nuclei, of activity around which land use patterns formed.

While Harris and Ullman still saw the CBD as the major center of commerce, they suggested that specialized cells of activity would develop according to specific requirements of certain activities, different rent-paying abilities, and the tendency for some kinds of economic activity to cluster together. At the center of their model is the CBD, with light manufacturing and wholesaling located along transport routes. Heavy industry was thought to locate near the outer edge of city, perhaps surrounded by lower-income households, and suburbs of commuters and smaller service centers would occupy the urban periphery.

The Multiple Nuclei Community Leadership Paradigm

Agenda For Autonomy

Before the idea for the New Kemet Plannign Bureau, it was in January of 1989, for instance, that I introduced what I called "The Agenda for Autonomy" on the radio in Milwaukee. In that proposal were ideas for a divestment campaign against area banks, a child care "development initiative," the creation of an Inner City Fundraising Council, a "broadcast music initiative" for young people, a "cultural consultants commission" to address school concerns (similar to the one I had proposed before the Omaha Public Schools back in 1980), and a "housing lottery" proposal. I left 25 copies at the front desk of the Courier and before the end of the day, they were all gone.

As stated. in the multiple nuclei model, the city consists of several different areas and as such, there may be more than one business district to serve these various areas.

Urban Planning and the African-American Community: In the Shadows

The following analysis and review of this important article also provides reasoning and rationale for my Africentric Sociourban Planning paradigm. The article is a review of a book, Urban Planning in the African American Community In the Shadows. The book is by June Thomas Manning and Marsha Ritzdorf and was published in 1997. The following snippet from the book is important regardless of the fact that the book is 21 years old. Scholarship is scholarship. Following then, are my analyses of this important work.

The review begins thusly:

> If urban planning is to **support the equitable distribution of public goods and services,** it must recognize **and address the dismal conditions of millions of Americans who are poor or people of color**. (Manning & Ritzdorf: 1997 – emphasis added).

There are two gross misconceptions in the previous excerpt.

The first one is that urban planning has some kind of obligation to "support the equitable distribution of public goods and services." Says who? Since when does a capitalist system have an obligation to give a damn about it's "have-nots" unless the end result was the creation of a new revenue stream? Answer: such a system has not nor will it ever.

Secondly since when does said system "address the dismal conditions of millions of Americans who are poor or people of color"? Answer: It does not because this set of conditions is inextricably bound to the "revenue stream" component and mandate alluded to in condition number one. In other words, if the poor and locked out do not represent a profit of some kind (tangible asset), then they become the antithesis of the capitalist vision and outcome: crippling liabilities.

What is about to be described serves as the basis and focus of my proposed Africentric Sociourban Planning paradigm. In fitting my proposal like a glove, the authors of the article offer the following:

> The primary focus of contemporary planners and planning students **should be on finding and advocating solutions that help eliminate the problems of today's cities**. Any meaningful solution will need to be **grounded in a thorough understanding of the race, gender, and class inequalities of American life**. (Manning & Ritzdorf, 1997 – emphasis added).

"Should be," the excerpt states. Will need to be", it adds. Let's talk about what actually IS.

What actually is revolves around the fact that expecting urban planners, as taught and constituted, to acquire a "thorough understanding of the race, gender, and class inequalities of American life" would be like expecting a wino to invent a laser beam. As constituted, the urban planning community is a reflection and reinforcement of those who came before them: land grabbing white nationalists who are more committed to segregation than salvation; more geared toward revenue streams than reality alterations; and surely more astute at maintaining the system than working to usher in a better and more equitable social reality.

That is where my Africentric Sociourban Planning paradigm comes into focus because it meets the shortcomings of traditional urban planning. That is partly because,

> One of the most significant and dramatic stories in the history of twentieth-century U.S. cities has been the growth and evolution of the African American population. In the early 1900s, the African American population was **simply one of many ethnic and racial groups living in U.S. cities** ... (Manning & Ritzdorf, 1997 – emphasis added).

Not only the growth and evolution of the African American population, but the courageous migration of same. In my book Exodus (2017, CreateSpace), I document the migration from south to north of black people and what they faced when the thought they had "escaped" the tribulations of the South only to have to deal with a more upbeat and urban set of discriminatory realities once they reached the north. That 350 year enslavement period and subsequent movement across the United States is one of the most incredible stories in human history on its own.

As a result we are not "simply one of many ethnic and racial groups living in U.S. cities." We gave form and function to the city, the fear of our people ushered in the white man's formation of today's police force, we forced a racist government to end Jim Crow laws and to at least pretend as if it believed in "civil rights." That is what black people represent. And anything short of that is an insult to the greatest race of people in the history of the world, plain and simple.

Moving right along:

> **African Americans became so visible in many central cities that some scholars defined their predominance and spatial isolation indications of city decline**. Indeed, throughout the twentieth century, racial prejudice shaped the lives of Blacks as surely as it shaped metropolitan areas. **Long after officially sanctioned racial prejudice subsided, racial oppression and inequality lingered.** Poverty grew more concentrated, and the quality of social life unraveled. **Physical deterioration became the norm.** (Manning & Ritzdorf, 1997 – emphasis added).

White scholars, no matter how unbiased or "objective" they believe themselves to be, simply cannot bear to tell the whole truth about the atrocities that were heaped upon the heads of black people by other white people. There is always, one way or another, the use of euphemism, downplaying, dilution, narrowing, decreasing or modifying their heinous, bellicose and nearly non-stop abuse of the black community. The previous paragraph is an example.

For instance, the use of "some scholars" defining black predominance as indications of decline. If "some" means "all white scholars with black scholars knowing better," then it would have been an accurate statement. But the white mindset is one that deals in extremes and when it comes to issues of race, a black influx that grows is equated with a "stain" on white supremacy. And that belief is reflected in their writings, policies and procedures.

Take note of the following bullshit claim: "Long after officially sanctioned racial prejudice subsided, racial oppression and inequality lingered." What?? That "officially sanctioned racial prejudice" was white racism, to define it accurately. It was "race hate," to give it a name. And when did it ever "subside"? White people have not changed in their views of black people and that can be seen in the daily language they use where a "black cat" still brings bad luck while a "white lie" is totally acceptable. White racism never subsided – it just switched gears to remain in line with the technological advances of the times.

Evidence can be find in the following line where the authors admit that poverty grew and the quality of black life unraveled and as a result, "physical deterioration became the norm." The fact is, since all of this was based on a white design and strategy, white intent and motivation, these realities are not separate or mutually exclusive; they are interdependent and overlapping parts of a master plan.

The African American community remained "in the shadows," to use the terminology of the author. And again, urban planning and land control were key cogs in the white supremacy machine:

> The twentieth century also **witnessed the evolution of professions that were dedicated to improving urban life and reducing urban decline.** Prominent among these was **urban planning.** Branching off from the municipal reform movement, and **away from the social work and housing reform movements,** urban planning aimed to create well-planned, orderly cities that allowed people to live free of slums, blight, and physical disorder. As the planning profession evolved, its practitioners **attacked various maladies affecting urban areas**. They joined efforts to remedy social problems, and they created initiatives designed to redevelop specific areas, such as the central business districts. (Manning & Ritzdorf, 1997 – emphasis added)

More revisionist assessments that need correction. So here we go with four major concerns and corrections.

To begin with the "evolution of professions" really mean the progress that paid positions went through and were created for. If your priority is the city and its land, then that is the type of professions that are going to be created. This does not mean the fair distribution of land because the white man stole it for one key reason: to horde all the land for himself and to make money in the process of doing so.

Since that is the case, then the "evolution" had nothing to do with "improving urban life" for anyone but his own race. And it only became "urban" after he washed his ass and began to form large enclaves in such a way that urban life and technology combined to create the concept of "city." Black people came along later and merely added the type of "urban flavor" that you see today. But that was resisted at the outset because the city was seen in the same way that Ronald Reagan saw this racist nation: "as a shining light upon the hill."

Improving urban life and "reducing urban decline" are euphemisms. As stated, improving urban life meant making way for increasing numbers of white to congregate. That meant new buildings, better streets, lighting and a sewer system. But the "urban decline" element meant addressing the issues of "class" because city dwellers were the well-to-do white folks. They didn't like or appreciate white immigrants and they surely had no room for people of color. Therefore "slums" were created the way today's junkyards and garbage dumps are reserved for the refuse and trash that people throw out. "Reducing urban decline" meant segregating by class and making sure that above all things, "the niggers knew their place."

Secondly, the claim that "urban planning" was among the professions that was geared toward addressing the aforementioned improvements and the addressing of urban decline. Again, urban planning was the brains of the racist robot, a robot who had a "Danger, Will Robinson" message ingrained on its computer screen whenever any person of color dare venture into a city area, dared to walk on "their" sidewalks" or sit in one of "their" parks. The urban planner is the one who laid out the code enforcements, who worked with banks to create redlining and steering strategies, and who ensured that the "slums" would be outside of the view of the everyday white person. And beyond the pale of human understanding as well.

Third, this is where the previous claim of the move "from the social work and housing reform movements" came into play. Social work was aimed at addressing the issues of incoming immigrants, low income people and the need for housing. The key was to control and clean up the slums where and when possible. This was not about benevolence of any kind. Social workers were just as racist as any other "profession," and these poverty snitches acted like police when it came to monitoring the poor and turning them in whenever possible. As for housing reform, that would come later on once the need for institutional residential segregation was endorsed and enforced with funding from the federal government.

Fourth and finally is the claim that, "As the planning profession evolved, its practitioners attacked various maladies affecting urban areas." This is straight-up bullshit. The truth of the matter is, the situation was the polar opposite: urban planners fomented, fanned and worked to maintain "maladies" affecting urban areas. And they did so because it was a land control issue and such patterns of segregation positively impacted the revenue stream. Later they would work out financial ways to maintain housing segregation by disguising it as if it was "affordable housing for low income." That lie persists to this very day.

According to the authors, "From the early part of the century, **when planning focused on creating land use controls and regulating growth,** to the end, when planners did these things plus many more, the profession's stated goal was to improve the experience of urban life for all residents. However, the reality was often far different**" (Manning & Ritzdorf, 1997 – emphasis added).

The reality is always "far different" once the variable of "race" has been interjected into the equation! These white people have these utopian ideas and then the question that delays their bullshit and selfish quest is "but what are we going to do about the niggers"? They can never build everything the same for everybody because that would put blacks and other people of color on equal footing with them. There has to be a class standing where blacks cannot dream of moving in and where they will, at the same time, feel comfortable being "relegated" or redlined into certain areas of the city. You can tell what area that is by the address numbers, the zip code and the street name.

So when the excerpt claims that land use controls were about regulating growth, the fact is that they were also about regulating population interaction. They were about segregation and maintaining it. That's why the paragraph also states that the "goal was to improve the experience of urban life for all residents." When blacks and whites are separate, whites are happy and black people can accept it. It wasn't until Martin Luther King, Jr., and the integration happy civil rights Negroes came staggering along begging for inclusion that things went out of whack. Segregation is externally imposed by whites on everyone else; separation, on the other hand, is mutually agreed upon.

Continuing:

> Throughout the twentieth century, the community of urban African Americans **connected with** the community of urban planning professionals. **At times those connections were sources of conflict and oppression, at other times sources of reform and cooperation.** Planning tools were and are often used **for the purpose of racial segregation.** Examples are **exclusionary zoning laws** and separatist **public housing programs.** Urban renewal **clearance projects** that bulldozed black communities into oblivion **could also be classified** as oppressive. (Manning & Ritzdorf, 1997 – emphasis added).

The first sentence is a distorted truth. Black communities "connected" with urban planning professionals in the same way that the guinea pig "connects" with the scientist and his experiments. That is all we ever were: black people on a giant Petri dish that white people could "observe," "monitor" and "evaluate." To also claim that "at times those connections were sources of conflict and oppression" is a gross understatement. So few were times where there was not conflict that they are not even worthy of mention. In other words, conflict between the planners and those being "planned for" was continual and it was harsh for the latter group.

What "sources of reform and cooperation" could these authors be referring to? By their own admission the concept of "exclusionary zoning" was on the books almost right away. And what does that form of zoning entail? In short, it is "a process by which a neighborhood or town makes it de facto illegal for low-income — or at times even non-poor — people to live in a given area." Once that took place, the public housing programs were constructed right there in the ghetto or barrio to ensure that those who were locked in stayed that way. I have offered enough insight on urban renewal to make it clear that there were no well-intended program or projects that came out of the minds of those planners; hence, my proposed Africentric Sociourban Planning paradigm – for us, by us and with our long-term welfare at heart.

The article continues:

> But these were not the only interactions between the black urban population and the profession. **During the 1960s, collective public guilt generated basic changes in urban planning professionals as well as in national policies.** Some planners – **whose ranks gradually became more diversified racially** – dedicated their lives to fighting for the rights of the poor and distressed. Such dedication took the form of "social" or **"advocacy" planning, neighborhood planning, or equity planning.** (Manning & Ritzdorf, 1997 – emphasis added).

Several points of clarification.

First of all in response to the claim that it was a matter of "collective public guilt" that "generated basic changes in urban planning professionals and national policies." No. The public was AFRAID. Black people were kicking them in the ass socially, culturally and physically. Black people were burning the country down and demanding the civil rights that white folks claimed to believe in. Only when that took place did these white planners put down their martinis and pull in their extended pinkie fingers and start giving serious consideration to those who were on the lower rungs of society.

Secondly, the claim that the ranks of planners have become more racially diverse. That is bullshit. The ranks of planning departments are more diverse with more black secretaries, low level planners who make copies and push paperwork and people of that ilk. But the ranks of those doing the actual planning cannot said to be more diverse unless that diversity is reflected in the final decisions. And that's not taking place; it's status quo with a few "house negroes" being marched in to say "yessuh boss" and make it appear as if people of color had some serious input.

Third and finally, the issues of advocacy planning, neighborhood planning and equity planning. I addressed these briefly earlier because they are all nice-sounding, but when you look into the definitions, study the source and substance of each, you see that they are merely tied to the same system that created the problem in the first place. Advocacy planning is the system "taking the side" of the poor community, meaning that they speak FOR the community and not TO it. Neighborhood planning has the same approach where planners come in and offer "options" and "alternatives" to community groups which have already been defined and determined. And equity planning, as I wrote earlier, is not about equity when planners are working within government and are using (pre-existing) research to influence the opinions of people who look just like they look and who have the same goals (contractors, developers, land grabbers, etc.)

> The precise nature of this **dualistic relationship of conflict versus cooperation needs further clarification.** Few historians of urban African-Americans give full and impartial treatment to the role of urban planning. Few historians of U.S. urban planning acknowledge the full influence of race and racial injustice on the profession. **Contributions made by African American women to urban planning efforts are underappreciated.** (Manning & Ritzdorf, 1997 – emphasis added).

What was just written is part of the problem, not because of what was described but the mentality of the people who wrote it. They key flaw in the previous excerpt was referring to what was taking place as a "dualistic relationship of conflict versus cooperation." This is not a dualistic relationship – it is an overlapping one. You cannot have cooperation unless there is some type of conflict that has taken place or is anticipated to take place. Conflict is the result of people seeking cooperation on some level. They are not separate entities but over lapping realities. To view black versus white, up versus down, right versus wrong as opposites creates more conflict – these are like what the Japanese called "the complementarity of opposites." This is what "equanimity" is about.

Not mentioning people of color showed the need for it to take place. The absence of the black presence in the literature created a void that therefore needed to be filled. Even the racist white man knew that – but he made these omissions and oversights intentionally. That does not dismiss what I am saying; it merely shows how one plus one is not just two; in an enlightened way, "one plus one is a greater one."

What my Africentric Sociourban Paradigm is about is taking the leadership out of the top-heavy planning approach and replacing it with people of color, planners who engage in what William Ouchi (1979) would refer to as "bottoms up authority." We studied the Japanese "ringi system" in a planning course and Ouchi's book, *A Conceptual Framework for the Design of Organizational Control Mechanisms* was an essential part of it. This is the attitude behind the ASP – leadership by people of color FOR people of color with the future of a "browning of America" being inevitable. White people can no longer teach what they don't know and lead what they don't know.

Put another way,

> In general, what is needed is an overview of the **critical linkages between the urban planning profession and the nation's most visible racial minority.** Race and racial injustice influence all efforts to **improve urban society**. Urban planning, an active profession, purports

to help improve civic life in metropolitan areas. It cannot do so unless its practitioners **more clearly understand the historical connections between this people and this field**. (Manning & Ritzdorf, 1997 – emphasis added).

Tip-toeing around the truth and actually engaging in truthfulness are two different things. Analysis of what was written in the previous paragraph will bring this point home more fully, since the contents represent more of the former than the latter.

For instance the claim that was is needed is an overview "of the critical linkages between the urban planning profession and the nation's most visible racial minority." This was written in 1997 – some 21 years ago – and since that time the most visible racial minority are the Latinos. That is mainly because black men have been locked up, gunned down and isolated. But blacks and browns share the same dominant status when it comes to injecting racial fear into white folks.

In light of that, the "critical linkages" between the two groups – people of color and the urban planning profession – is nothing but a false ideal, a façade, a fake factoid. These people only see "linkages" in the way the farmer sees the mule pulling the plow. They cannot be trusted or, as the First Nation people taught, "The white man speaks with forked tongue."

In addition, a "more clearly understood historical connection between people of color and the urban planning field" is a waste of time. The essential understanding can be found merely in the observation of race relations in American society: peckerwoods on top, people of color on the bottom. When there is talk of a connection between the races, this most fundamental of facts must be understood: any talk of inclusion or diversity or any of the buzzwords (that really don't mean shit) is rooted in and revolves around the white planner calling the shots and dominating the program. That is why time has come for the Africentric Sociourban Paradigm. More on that later.

The article then moves into the area of "planning and public policy":

> The period after World War II saw two simultaneous processes: (1) the **movement of the White middle and working classes to the suburbs**, a movement spurred by the return of World War II veterans and the assistance of home mortgage insurance programs, and (2) **the consolidation of ghetto boundaries**. It is for this era that we have the best documentation concerning the relationship between African American urban life and planning decisions. (Manning & Ritzdorf, 1997 – emphasis added).

Notice the niceties of the terms that were just used. Let me break it down so that the reality of race relations can be better discerned: When the first point reads that the movement of the white middle class to the suburbs coincided with the second point, "the consolidation of ghetto boundaries," what is really meant is quite simple. White folks shouted, "The niggers are coming!" and ran for the suburbs and left the city behind. Of course they took the city services with them and that left the inner city virtually moribund. It was called "white flight," and planning decisions began being based on that cowardly reality.

Furthermore,

> As several scholars have demonstrated, **political leaders' desire to shape black residence patterns profoundly influenced public housing and urban renewal policies.** Just as urban migration of rural blacks and other ethnic minorities was the demographic motivation for racially exclusionary zoning and restrictive covenants during the period between the world wars, **the need to contain blacks in restricted sections of cities influenced public policy decisions after World War II.** (Manning & Ritzdorf, 1997 – emphasis added).

To begin with, the "desire" of political leaders to shape black residence patterns only influenced public housing and urban renewal policies insofar as those political leaders were leeching for federal dollars. They knew that if they compartmentalized the blacks and Latinos, if they forced them to live in high density areas and live on top of one another, they would be able to qualify for money to build multi-unit dwellings (public housing apartments) and maintain the segregated conditions at the government's expense. There is nothing benevolent about that, and once the money came in, more "government programs" were created to create even more free money for the city, inclusive of grants for the police to ensure that segregation was maintained: Urban Development Action Grants, Project Safe Neighborhoods, Project Triggerlock, Community Development Block Grants, Weed and Seed.

Put another way,

> The movement to the suburbs by the white middle and working classes, which one author calls **a true "metropolitan revolution,"** clearly established decentralization as the dominant urban pattern for the following decades. This decentralization, however, was exclusionary. For example, Levittown, New York, a well-known suburban community that set the pattern for numerous others, housed 82,000 residents in 1960, not one of whom was African American. **Although white families found new opportunities opening up in freshly constructed suburbs,** African American families experienced **disproportionate overcrowding and limited mobility within the central cities left behind.** (Manning & Ritzdorf, 1997 – emphasis added).

How can you have a "metropolitan revolution" when the status quo remained the same? Just because the land thieves have relocated and left the inner city to the "have-nots" does not make it a "revolutionary" act. A revolution is a total change of a system. This was more like a "racial rebellion" where cowardly white folks shook their pale fists and shouted "we'll show you!" as they scampered into suburbia and created a set of realities that totally excluded black people as residents. Of course black people who were left behind paid the rents on the houses that the whites left behind, which created a new revenue stream for the peckerwood.

The programs kept coming, as did the free money to assist in controlling the urban "slum":

> A series of federal policies set the stage for these conditions. Urban renewal was one of the most invidious. Often called "Negro removal" by critics, it provides countless examples of the interconnection of racial change with local policy. **Urban renewal** systematically destroyed many African American communities and businesses and, for most of its history, failed to safeguard the rights and well-being of those forcibly relocated from those homes and businesses. That clearance for urban renewal worked in conjunction with clearance for highway construction only made matters worse. **Backed by the federal government, cities simultaneously cleared out slums and displaced racial minorities from prime locations for redevelopment and highway construction. These policies shaped and defined the black ghetto.** (Manning & Ritzdorf, 1997 emphasis added).

Any black person that sat in on the meetings that allowed the feds to usher in urban renewal was nothing short of a bootlicking Uncle Tom. They saw what urban renewal was designed to do. Look at the major freeways across America: most of them cleave their way through some black area of town, dispersing black people and sabotaging black businesses. The rich got richer as the freeways expedited white travel from their suburban homes to the local airport, the riverfront or downtown –at the expense of black residents. They could look down their pointed noses at the ghetto they created and continue with their references to "those people."

The same people who blame riots for the destruction of ghetto buildings and business rarely want to mention the damage done by urban renewal and Model Cities. These white people just came in with their racist code enforcement and their land use rulings and destroyed entire blocks of black housing in the name of "progress." Now, after the fact, scholars like the writers of the article want to talk as if the riots were "a long time in coming" or were "deserved." But they weren't saying that shit then when we were running down the street throwing firebombs and kicking any white man's ass that was in the vicinity! The cry at that time was "somebody call a fuckin' cop!"

As Manning & Ritzdorf (1997) document it,

> The 1960s, **the era of civil rebellion**, brought several important changes. The widespread civil disorders, which were volatile but **predictable responses to long-standing racial oppression, forced significant alterations in federal policies**. President Lyndon Johnson, attempting to build a "Great Society," initiated new programs that focused on eliminating poverty and empowering low-income communities. With the **War on Poverty's community action agencies,** citizens gained the power to supervise community improvement directly. Under Model Cities, local citizen governing boards also helped direct local redevelopment and made their own contributions to the **redefinition of urban planning.** (emphasis added)

These urban planners just won't give a nigga a break. They call it "civil rebellion," but it was a "black rebellion" and they know and that is why they feared it and acted so quickly to quell it. And those "alterations in federal policy" were not all that significant because the power relations didn't change. The white man was still pulling the strings and black people were still the puppets, but the approach to control was more subtle. The white man still made the decisions, controlled the budgets, selected the black lackeys that would serve as the "buffer zone" and in doing all that proved that "as things change, so they remain the same."

War on poverty? Like the War on Drugs which was another scam that would be run, both ended up being "a war on black folks." Those community action agencies were a good idea and some of them handed out some "feel good" activities: doling out food stamps, handing out free cheese and butter, giving away clothes, helping with utility bills. All that pacification type bullshit. But the "action" that was exhibited was all geared toward endearing the oppressed to the same system that was the source of the problem. They put out newsletters and maybe opened a small black library here and there, but there was nothing done to address what was needed: power.

Model Cities didn't re-define urban planning: it exploited it with the same lies as would be the case with future urban renewal programs. Grandiose names giving black lackeys keys that didn't fit anything. And when these programs failed, blame was placed squarely on "those people" who "didn't know a good thing when they saw it."

The Housing and Community Development Act of 1974 killed the oppressive urban renewal program, but it also brought the

> **promising Model Cities experiment to a halt.** With the 1974 act, which created **Community Development Block Grants (CDBGs),** the federal government withdrew from **high-profile attempts** to target funds to distressed central-city efforts, defined and guided by local citizens. Instead, in city after city, **citizens who had just begun to exercise some control over the redevelopment of their neighborhoods experienced the shock of government withdrawal.** Although in later years the CDBG program somewhat improved on its record of participation, in general the program **placed decision making in the hands of city government** and dispersed national funding via a formula that spread increasingly scarce redevelopment funds to populous suburbs as well as to a wide range of cities. (Manning & Ritzdorf, 1997 – emphasis added).

Correction is in order so that the previous distortions can be clarified in terms of how all this relates to African-American people.

First off, the HCD Act of 1974 didn't kill any oppressive urban renewal programs or Model Cities. It merely changed the hands of the oppressor from the feds to the local city powers that be. And those cities couldn't wait to apply for and get that free money. Even hick cities like Omaha, Nebraska and those of similar size applied for and got that free money. All you needed to do to qualify was have what was called "a pocket of poverty" and most cities had long been maintaining one of those without actually referring to it as such. To most it was just a "slum," a "ghetto" or a "central city." Now, under the CDBG program, they could actually get paid for having one!

Secondly, those "high profile attempts" to target funds to the inner city fell far short – by design. Being high profile and being effective are two different things, and all those programs, from urban renewal and Model Cities to the vaunted CDBG program, all proved that to be the case. They were promoted in a way that made it appear as if they were "in control" of the ghetto. But in reality, all they did was create jobs for white folks and a few token negroes who accepted money under the table to keep their mouths shut. That is why they fell by the wayside.

Third, the claim that, "citizens who had just begun to exercise some control over the redevelopment of their neighborhoods experienced the shock of government withdrawal" is bullshit. There was never any feeling of "control over redevelopment" of the 'hood. There was the illusion that things were changing because white people were doling out crumbs in the guise of neighborhood watch, some brand new street lights, upgraded sewers and marching out a few coons in suits who claimed to be leaders. But nothing tangible took place which is why the ghetto, in many instances, is worse off today n 2018 than it was back in the 1970s and 1980s.

Fourth and finally, CDBG in the hands of city government was worse than before because it application of the funding was "discretionary." These white people got those funds and began spending it on suburban expansion, downtown development, riverfront recreation, parks and malls and so on. The ghetto got its money by way of a few token organizations that were nothing but "shills" for the city, manned by token negroes who knew nothing about development or urban planning, and who basically handed out tools, sponsored a few festivals and were present whenever the white man needed to make a presentation in front of ghetto residents.

> Previous efforts to mesh social, economic, and physical development strategies, a mixture allowed under Model Cities, succumbed under the **pervasive "bricks and mortar" orientation of the CDBG program**. Any illusions that inner-city residents might have had that a benign federal government would "gild" their ghetto **died quickly with the unstable funding, unpredictable longevity, and strong downtown focus that characterized urban-related programs such as action grants and economic development assistance funds in the 1970s, 1980s, and early 1990s.** The mid-1990s brought promising federal program initiatives, such as **Empowerment Zones/Enterprise Communities.** But by that time African American families, even those in suburbia, **remained highly segregated**. They earned less money than others per capita and per family, and experienced much narrower options of residence than did other Americans. (Manning & Ritzdorf, 1997).

What goes in is what comes out. White people are not capable of treating people of color fairly. It is not in their DNA – simply look at urban history.

For instance, in the previous excerpt the claim is made that previous programs "succumbed under the pervasive "bricks and mortar" orientation of the CDBG program." Those previous programs were already dead; the bricks and mortar orientation of CDBG came about after a lie was told that money, in the hands of city leaders, would do a much better job than the federal "projects" that had failed so miserably in the past (by design). It was a classic case of one hand washing the other.

If any inner city residents believed that the government would "gild" their ghetto, they should have had their black asses kicked. How can you trust benevolence from someone who has, for over 300 years, proven to be your bitter enemy? But these writers make the claim that the illusions of residents "died quickly with the unstable funding, unpredictable longevity, and strong downtown focus that characterized urban-related programs such as action grants and economic development assistance funds in the 1970s, 1980s, and early 1990s." We should have seen it coming.

The fact that the ghetto, despite the coming of so-called "community development block grants" remained concentrated and impoverished should have been no surprise. The funding was being steered elsewhere

Constitutional and Legal Issues of Urban Planning and Land Use Control: An Urban Geography Analysis

From a book called *Contemporary Urban Planning* by John M. Levy, we find information on urban geography. My job is to relate it to the Africentric Sociourban Paradigm and how this information impacts upon and can improve the black community.

> The framers of the U.S. Constitution in 1787 could scarcely have foreseen that the United States would eventually be a "nation of cities", in the phrase of historian Sam Bass Warner (1966) (p. 252)

The framers of the Constitution, as we now know, were members of the elite, and were white and male. Based upon that fact alone, one can hardly question how "inclusive" they were when they were "foreseeing" what they believed America would become. One thing was for sure; they held slaves and, for the most part, believed that those individuals were inferior. So it matters little about what they produce because we know that the mind dictates actions. If one believes that the races should be separate – and these men surely believed that – then the institutions, policies and procedures produced by these men will reinforce that belief. That's the way it was with the Founding Fathers, and that's the way it appears to be today with city administrations, planning departments and planners themselves – especially as those "plans" relate to how land will be used.

Moving on,

> Procedural due process "centers not so much on what is done but on how it has been done" … Substantive due process … concerns the purpose of the government action, while the taking issue considers it economic impact (Levy, p. 253)

As it relates to substantive due process, the judge declared a scathing indictment of zoning based on substantive due process and equal protection grounds when he said, in part, "In the last analysis, the result to be accomplished is to classify the population and segregate them according to their income or situation in life." (p. 262)

The article claims that, "If this opinion had been upheld by the U.S. Supreme Court, the face of metropolitan America might look rather different today. However it was reversed" (Levy, p. 262) How might it look different? Is America not, indeed, residentially and racially segregated?

America is already segregated by income and "situation in life," and that is the case despite a plethora of civil rights laws, housing decisions, rules and regulations prohibiting steering, redlining and blockbusting and remains the case whether the governing administration is liberal, moderate or conservative. Again, the issue of "race" is one that should be discussed more when it comes to land use planning because, as W.E.B. DuBois wrote, "the problem of the 20th Century is the problem of the color line." And this remains true even in this, the 21st Century.

THE ISSUE OF ZONING AND "TAKING"

While the information on billboard regulations (p. 288) and historic preservation laws and the relationship of both of these subjects to planning was insightful, I was particularly interested in zoning, the police power and the legal rulings which governed these two important forms of land use control. I am further interested in the issue of land use control when the variable of "race" becomes a part of the equation.

The land use article continues by claiming:

> The most enduring issue confronting zoning and other land use regulation is the "taking issue" – to what extent can regulations reduce the value of private property without compensation to the owner? (p. 258)

This is only an "issue" when the person whose land is being taken is minority, low income or politically unsophisticated. The taking of land of those considered "different" is a long-time American tradition which began with the taking of land from the members of the indigenous population. From that point on, the taking of land was a matter of who had the most money, the most guns, the most power. This was the case prior to "regulations" and now, in a more technologically astute America, remains the case if the person is not aware, does not have good legal representation and depending on how badly the government wants the land. With the advent of Eminent Domain, those in power still have the right to take land whenever they want to, and need only show that it serves "the public good" – meaning the well-being of those in the majority.

> Where private property is deliberately taken for a public use or purpose,
> as for streets, parks or schools, the public authority clearly must pay the
> private owner "just compensation." This means fair market value as
> established by a jury (p. 259).

"Just compensation" according to prices and estimates put together by individuals who intentionally devalue the land in certain areas of the city. That is why those in power flex their muscles in these areas. Freeways are rammed through poor areas and "developments" are forced into these areas because the land is cheap based on real estate values. If the area is black, the land is said to be worth less than in an area that is white and suburban. How can this be? Land is land. But since this is the case, "fair and just compensation" means more to the suburbanite than to the central city resident, even though both may be homeowners.

Put another way,

> On the other hand, zoning necessarily reduces some property
> values by limiting the range of choice and manner in which the
> property may be developed and utilized. Should such reduction in
> the value of some property for the benefit of others be
> compensable? (p. 259)

This is but one form of property value reduction. What about the reductions based on race of the people who live in that area? It exists all over America, from the largest cities to the middle sized cities, anywhere where there exists a "pocket of poverty."

The police power and zoning, then, do not work the same in all parts of the city. They are not applied the same or ruled in the same in courts of law. Poor people do not receive the same kind of justice as those who have money, and there are hundreds, if not thousands, of studies which show that this is the case. America is based on the ceaseless pursuit of profit, and this extends into the area of real estate and, as a result, into the minds and habits of those who are planners and who assist in making planning decisions.

ZONING AND THE LAND QUESTION

The issue of zoning is one which is controversial when the variable of "race" is interjected. The article stated, "Zoning is a tool in the hands of governmental bodies which enables them to more efficiently meet the demands of evolving and growing communities … Zoning provisions may not be used … to avoid the increased responsibilities and economic burdens which time and natural growth invariably bring" (p. 275)

> The early period of zoning was marked by a paradox concerning aesthetics. On the one hand, the basic terms of Euclidian zoning – segregation of uses, minimum lot size, setbacks, and so forth – are inherently aesthetic in nature. They embody the aesthetic of the turn-of-the-century garden suburb: single-family detached homes with spacious, landscaped from yards set back evenly from the street with nonresidential activities banished from the area (p. 285).

My point regarding the significance of race is even echoed by the author when he cites the case of *Southern Burlington County NAACP v. Township of Mount Laurel 336 A.2d 713, 1975*, and it figures that the NAACP would be involved and bring the issue of race into play. If they didn't do it, the planners certainly would not have. At any rate, it was found that Mount Laurel wanted to control growth by accepting a certain kind of population (white folks) and that "through its zoning ordinances has exhibited economic discrimination in that the poor have been deprived of adequate housing, and has used federal, state, county, and local finances and resources solely for the betterment of middle- and upper-income persons" (p. 277).

And, "the opinion explicitly raises FOR PERHAPS THE FIRST TIME the constitutional issue as to "whose general welfare must be served or not violated in the field of land use regulation" (p. 277). We should remember the words of Justice William O. Douglas when he wrote what I consider to be a racist definition of aesthetic in planning:

> The concept of the public welfare is broad and inclusive … The values it represents are spiritual as well as physical, aesthetic as well as monetary. It is within the power of the legislature to determine that the community should be beautiful as well as healthy, spacious as well as clean, well-balanced as well as carefully patrolled … If those who govern the District of Columbia decide that the Nation's Capitol should be beautiful as well as sanitary there is nothing in the Fifth Amendment that stands in the way (75S.Ct.at 102-103).

All communities should be spacious and beautiful and sanitary, should they not? Therefore, by delineating above about the legislature having the power "to determine" that the community should be those things, it is clear that some communities should, and some communities should not. If this was not the case, then every community would look the same, have the same access to services and be provided with the same resources. But are they? No. And whose fault is it? It is the fault of the legislatures who allocate money and the cities who take money earmarked for poor areas and spend it developing suburbs and exurbs and downtowns.

The Mount Laurel case opened up the issue of discrimination and race and some good things came out of it, including making every municipality provide lower cost housing opportunities for its resident poor, and the formation of a special panel of judges and using affirmative action to provide low-cost housing (p. 279). The Mount Laurel case also led to the establishment of a Council on Affordable Housing and provided a mediation and review process.

Zoning and the issue of "reason" are some times difficult to understand. It is explained as follows:

> "Reasonableness" is thus often used as a surrogate for "constitutionality." Although it may beg the questions, reasonableness has provided a convenient rubric for courts to resolve zoning challenges. The inquiry takes the following form: Is the ordinance reasonably related to a valid purpose of the police power and does it reserve for the owner some reasonable way to use the property (although not necessarily the most profitable one)? (p. 255)

What is "valid" for those in power is, in far too many cases, "invalid" to those who are being imposed upon. The majority rules and although minorities are said to have rights, those rights are overridden when it comes to the police power. The concept of "reasonableness" is based upon what those in the majority view as being valid and how the majority benefits from the way the property is used. This is why freeways continue to go through poor and minority communities, destroying entire subcultures. North Omaha is but one example of how the police power and how the rights of suburbanites and their need to expedite the trip from the Eppley Airfield to West Omaha was deemed more "reasonable" than the rights of the poor and the number of low-income housing units that were destroyed to make way for the interstate.

It all appears arbitrary to me. The article claims,

> After nearly four decades of national experience with zoning, Haar … reported: "For the most part, however, zoning has preceded planning in the communities which now provide for the latter activity, and indeed, nearly one-half of the cities with comprehensive zoning ordinances have not adopted master plans at all … (p. 257)

In my view, zoning IS planning; it plans for business and residences to combine when it is in the best interests of the community. It is a combination of what the residents want and what is best for their kids. But then when "others" move in, zoning is used to segregate and alienate. Planners then come into the picture, not to do the right thing and undo the wrong that was committed – but to justify and strengthen those wrongs! This partially explains the following excerpt:

> Bettman argued that modern urban development was producing unprecedented problems of congestion and inefficiency. He argued that orderliness of land usage pursuant to a master plan is a proper use of the police power (p. 263)

Modern urban development is as racist as the people who abused the white ethnics coming into the cities. Following the compartmentalization of those people, and watching while the sewers backed up and health problems killed many of them, the modern urban development then allowed the newly arriving blacks to experience the same congestion and health problems. "Orderliness of land use," at least in my view, was reserved for the well-to-do and later, for those whites who were fleeing the inner cities to head for the suburbs.

> In the case of *Nollan v. California Coastal Commission 107S.Ct. 3141, 1987, "* … a restriction on a rebuilding permit for an oceanfront home that required the owners to allow the public an easement to walk along the dry sand (private) portion of the beach in front of their home. This was consistent with similar restrictions placed on new and rebuilt shorefront by the Commission to promote public access along beaches…"(p. 265)

The court ruled that if California wanted an easement across the Nollans' property, then the state must pay for it. This case "thus reflected a long-standing doctrine that the police power may properly be used to prevent public harm but not to confer public benefits without compensation" (p. 265). But just the fact that there was an "assumption" that this could become law shows the arrogance and subtle underhandedness of zoning administrators and planners. For a less politically sophisticated community in a less desirable social and geographic setting, such one-sided laws would perhaps not be stifled by the courts.

In *Lucas v. South Carolina Coastal Council 112 S.Ct.2886, 1992,* the issue of fair compensation for the taking of land was addressed and while a trial court agreed and awarded Lucas $1.2 million for his beach front property, The South Carolina Supreme Court reversed the trial court, holding the permit denial to be a valid application of the police power … (p. 266).

Zoning supports those who have the money to afford good legal defense. But what about the poor and how does zoning operate when the variable of "race" comes into play? In my view, all three types of zoning cited on page 270 have the potential for being racist when the variable of "race" comes into play.

For instance, exclusionary zoning is "the use of zoning to deter construction of homes or siting of mobile homes for moderate-income families or members of racial or other minorities." Recently in the Omaha World Herald, there was an article in the August 4, 2000 issue of the paper under the headline, "Judge Says Town Has Racist Zoning." It appears that in Sunnyvale, Texas, "A federal judge has ruled that leaders in the predominantly white Dallas suburb have been shutting out minorities and the poor for 50 years through illegal zoning laws." Continuing:

> Sunnyvale Mayor Jim Phaup said the city may appeal the ruling. He disputed Bachmeyer's allegation that the city of about 3,000 was formed to exclude minorities. "It's all about open spaces and country fields. It has nothing to do with discriminatory practices," Phaup says (Omaha World Herald, p. 11).

It has to do with white racism and that is evidenced by the following excerpt:

> Reggie Smith, a plaintiff in the lawsuit, said his construction company tried unsuccessfully in 1988 to build affordable homes and apartments in Sunnyvale. He said he overheard racial slurs during public meetings regarding his application. Urban experts say regulating for size or square footage of homes is exclusionary because it drives up the cost of a home. But few such zoning practices have been challenged in federal court , said David Rusk, a former Albuquerque mayor and author of a book examining the social costs of exclusionary zoning (Omaha World Herald, p. 11).

I'm not concerned about the racial slurs that Smith claims he heard at the meetings. Since he didn't bother to address them or deal with them, then he is just another "quiet nigger" in my book.

But my concern is that the article talks of "urban experts" who talk of regulating the size or square footage of homes being exclusionary. Why can't "planners" do it? Why WON'T planners do it? Why does it take a former mayor to write a book on "exclusionary zoning"? I'll tell you why: because of the "politics" involved in planning, that's why. The Planning Department serves the existing political order or lives off of the government dole through funding from the office of Housing and Urban Development. Those planners see racist actions, ordinances, variances and proposals before them every day, but they don't act unless the action is in accord with the existing power structure.

Frederick Law Olmstead, the man who built New York's Central Park, faced it in his day, and it's still going on. Without the "urban experts" around – people like Douglass Massey and Nancy Denton (who co-wrote "American Apartheid"), Peter Suzuki (the director of UNOs Urban Studies program) and the like – the urban planners would be running amok on poor communities and doing the racist bidding of whatever the power structure dictates.

In regard to Fiscal zoning, it is defined on page 270 of the urban planning article as, "the use of zoning to minimize local property taxes by encouraging revenue generating activities such as shopping centers and industrial parks while discouraging revenue-demanding uses such as lower-cost homes for families with children (regardless of race)."

This is exactly what is happening in North Omaha right now. Placing an industrial park in an area where businesses are nil and where people are poor. Why? To keep the property taxes elsewhere, down. At the same time, lower-cost homes are torn down to pave the way for the North Freeway, and expensive homes such as those being built by Michael Maroney in his "Concord Townhomes" project, are being given preferential treatment. Why? To attract yuppies and others who have the financial power back into the central city, near downtown where the real jobs are. Commute time gets cut down, the area is "re-taken" by the whites who fled in the 1960s and blacks are relocated to the northwestern sector of the area.

Finally, NIMBY, which stands for "not in my back yard." This form of zoning and other legal means are used to "resist the location of unwanted uses, facilities, or activities within the municipality (such as regional incinerators or toxic waste disposal sites, prisons, mental health facilities, oil refineries, public housing).

But NIMBY is good for some and bad for others. After all, where are those toxic waste disposal sites, garbage dumps, packing houses, prisons and public housing placed? Either in a rural area or in or near a central city. For the most part the rural areas get the prisons because politicians want those areas to have jobs. In addition, the prison population is considered and counted as part of the congressional district, although the prisoners cannot vote. Meanwhile, the central cities get the toxic disposal sites, such as ASARCO (right near North Omaha in the downtown area) and even now it is discovered that there is toxic land on the site that was formerly Druid Hill Elementary School. "Not in my back yard," for the most part, has come to mean "put it in the low-income area" and poison THOSE people, not our suburban kids.

Finally in 1986 the assumption for the responsibility for housing policy diluted the impact of the courts and placed the power in the hands of state legislatures. According to one scholar, the courts were ill-suited and inappropriate forums to resolve technical housing issues (p. 280). Not just the technical issues – the social ones as well.

Not that the legislatures are doing any better. Look at the Nebraska situation: is North Omaha faring any better just because the legislature exists? North Omaha looks worse NOW than it did twenty years ago. So the courts might be out of touch and may be ill-suited, but the same can be said about the legislature when it comes to the black community. After all, the abuse of HUD monies by the city of Omaha had to be approved by the state HUD office, and the legislators had to know about the projects that were being prioritized and the amount of money allocated to the state.

The "essence of the issue is which public is implied in constitutional protection of the "general welfare" – the strictly local public, or the larger publics of the region, state, nation or globe?" (p. 270) I have a feeling that the 'public' being defined is not based on geographic size, but on numbers and race. In this context, "general welfare" comes to mean the welfare of the "general public," the majority of people. This comes to mean the white majority here in America. This is seen in why freeways don't go through suburban housing districts, why toxic waste is stored in low-income areas, why low-income housing is placed in low-income areas creating economic re-segregation and why racial segregation continues to exist in America. The "general public" means the white majority, pure and simple.

In the sub-chapter of "Urban Housing for the Poor," evidence of racism and concern for the "general welfare" of the public becomes most evident:

> While housing activists labored to open the suburbs to affordable housing, existing stocks of older housing in the central cities continued to decline During the 1950s and 1960s, efforts to save or replace urban housing followed two general approaches: public housing and urban renewal. Both involved a partnership of federal funding and technical guidance with local administration. Both approaches were to be challenged as ineffective and counterproductive (p. 281).

If they were "challenged as ineffective and counterproductive" then they must have been ineffective and counterproductive, right? Why can't the author bring himself to say that? Those of us who are minority who watched as housing went down and was not replaced, KNOW well that urban renewal basically meant, "Negro removal."

HOUSING PROGRAMS AND THE CENTRAL CITY

Secondly, if the approaches of public housing and urban renewal did not work, then whose fault is that and why were the programs continually re-funded? Why does it take five or ten years for the government to "find out" that something is "failing" in the central city? The answer is because the people who make up the government – local, state or national – do not live in these central city areas for the most part. They live OUTSIDE of the area and once they leave their jobs, they really don't care how the plan goes. After all, jobs are being created and the economy is expanding, and that means votes. But the people who are supposed to benefit are being "experimented on" with these approaches and if it works, fine but if it doesn't work, those in power don't really have to worry about facing any repercussions.

The mistakes are made because those coming up with these ideas don't really care about the end result. Then, when the failure does take place, scholars and urban planners come along to "intellectually explain away" what took place. A case in point appears in the following passage:

> Congress established the Slum Clearance Program for replacement of tenements with publicly owned housing projects … Many public housing units were uninhabitable by the mid-1960s due to inappropriate design, isolated location, occupancy policies, and lack of upkeep (p. 281).

This is what happened in Omaha when Aulden Aust, the former director of city planning, decided to destroy hundreds of houses in North Omaha, claiming that they were paving the way for Urban Renewal. Later, he would say that this was a mistake, that those houses could have been renovated. But what do we have: a mistake made at the expense of people who are not politically sophisticated, who are poor and who are minority. So what if a mistake is made? Does anybody care enough to punish the government for destroying black lives?

How can a program that includes housing units which were not designed appropriately, that were built in isolated locations (far from jobs and community), contained discriminatory occupancy policies and lacked upkeep from those hired to do just that, how can a program like this go unpunished? How can the formulators continue to find jobs as urban planners? How can history downplay the destruction and devastation that blacks and other minorities had to face while these "programs" came and failed? Who speaks for the poor?

For example, take St. Louis:

> The infamous Pruitt-Igoe Project in St. Louis, for example, consisted of 43
> eleven-story buildings. By 1970, 26 of these were boarded up, and in 1972 all
> were demolished by the city's housing authority (p. 282).

What about the insanity that took place in and around the Robert Taylor Homes and the Cabrini-Green Housing projects in Chicago? What about the failures of high rises all over the nation and people being burned up in them? Elevators failing? Taken over by gangs? A major waste of taxpayers money because someone wanted to "experiment." They figured that by going up in the air (building multi-story buildings) they could build more units and use less actual land. There are no high-rise projects in white suburban communities. Even the high rise hotels have zoning limits placed on them. So once again we have different levels of priority and concern based upon the income and the race of the resident population.

Race not a factor? It becomes clear when those in the suburbs and those with political power want to concentrate and segregated people based upon race. The following excerpt bears out this allegation:

> Aside from poor design, a fundamental objection of civil rights
> advocates to federal public housing policy was the practice of
> locating most projects (except elderly housing) in black ghetto
> areas, thus reinforcing patterns of racial segregation since most
> occupants were nonwhite. In a suit filed by the NAACP, the
> federal district court of Chicago held that this practice violated the
> Fourteenth Amendment and ordered new public housing to be
> scattered in small clusters throughout the city (p. 282).

Why did it take "civil rights" advocates to expose a problem that was created by urban planners and "experts"? Why did it take civil rights activists to see that those in power were "re-segregating" the American social landscape? The answer is clear and it shows that once the variable of "race" is interjected into the "plan," the same rules and regulations which apply to the "general population" and for the "general welfare" usually don't apply for any number of reasons. We need only look at the issue of land use, as we are doing now, to see that this allegation has historical precedent and continues on to this day.

How else to explain the resistance to "scattered-site housing" by these Omaha suburbanites? Where is the scattered site housing going, for the most part? Right into North Omaha. There are some sites elsewhere in Omaha, but the white community groups got the city to change the design and the locations and basically turned the low-income houses into condos of sorts. But this was the exception, not the rule. One need only attend a city council meeting when the issue of low-income housing arises to see residents coming out and using the myth of "lowered property values." Laurenti debunked that lie more than three decades ago. It only continues to exist because those in the suburbs continue to want segregation from people who are different.

Why does it take community activists and civil rights advocates to point out this racialist issues? Part of the answer can be found in the following paragraph:

> The record of federal involvement in housing for the poor, however, has generally been shameful in comparison with the many forms of federal subsidy to the habitability of middle- and upper-class suburbs (p. 282).

In the vernacular of the ghetto, "different strokes for different folks." And while the preceding excerpt makes it appears as if the dichotomy is based on housing for the poor versus middle and upper-class suburbs, the issue is really centered on the people who make up these two areas. When stripped of its pomp and ceremony, the issue is low income versus well-to-do, minority versus non-minority.

And since the issue was one of race, for the most part, it only stands to reason that racism would be an integral part of the process – keeping minorities down and out of the way. Urban Renewal was but one example of that:

> The federal Urban Renewal Program was also widely discredited. Under the Housing Acts of 1949 and 1954, urban renewal funded local authorities to plan, acquire, clear and redevelop designated areas of "urban blight." With the approval of the <u>U.S. Supreme Court in Berman v. Parker</u> in 1954 … the program cleared thousands of acres of inner-city tenements and displaced tens of thousands of low-income households and small businesses. Aside from the areas rebuilt with public facilities such as schools and parks, most urban renewal land was sold at a subsidized price to private redevelopers to be reused according to the urban renewal plan (pp. 282-283).

The private developers benefited, the city that received the money benefited, many people were employed as part of the program (more non-minorities than minorities, no doubt) and the program was a feather in the cap of whomever claimed to be about "helping the poor." But even the most conservative planner has to admit that major displacement of populations took place, and poor people lost their homes and their livelihoods in the name of "progress" that never really took place.

Now, in retrospect, everybody wants to be a moralist or a critic:

> Urban renewal was attacked from several standpoints. Housing
> advocates complained that poor people displaced by the projects
> could not afford the new units built the same sites and were given
> little help in finding alternative housing … Also, there was no
> compensation by urban renewal authorities to displaced tenants
> and small businesses … In response to these criticisms, the Federal
> Uniform Relocation Assistance Act of 1970 authorized grants and
> relocation assistance to households and businesses by federally
> funded projects (p. 283).

At first there was no compensation to those who were relocated or displaced. But the fact of the matter is, even with the advent of the Federal Uniform Relocation Assistant Act of 1970 which gave out some grants and "relocation assistance," these funds were inadequate and the "assistance" was short-term: one-time only. So if you had a home that was paid for and you were relocated to an apartment, $10,000 was not only an underpayment for your home, but it would only last so long now that you are a renter, not an owner. And the "assistance" came in the form of "advice" and "referrals," not cash. In other words, most of those who were displaced ended up doing WORSE than they were doing before the government came in and took their homes and moved them away from an area where they had grown to feel comfortable.

The problems didn't only impact upon the hard-core slum dwellers, either:

> Others criticized the disruption of ethnically diverse urban
> neighborhoods and their replacement by sterile, unsafe high-rise
> development (p. 283).

Moving on,

> In 1965, Congress created the Department of Housing and Urban
> Development (HUD) as recommended by President Johnson's Task
> Force on Metropolitan and Urban Problems to serve as an umbrella for
> federal housing programs … In 1966, the Demonstration Cities and
> Metropolitan Development Act of 1966 launched the "Model Cities"
> program, which sought to upgrade community facilities, jobs and social
> programs in some 150 cities (p. 283).

Levy (2000) reminds us that, "In 1966, while its influence with Congress was still great, the Johnson administration had pushed through the Model Cities Program. Building upon long-established public housing and urban renewal efforts, Model Cities attempted to integrate physical redevelopment of inner city neighborhoods with a wide range of social services and job opportunities" (p. 100). Model Cities failed just as other programs before it had failed. But were the people fired? Were they banned from ever practicing their trades as planners, engineers or theorists? No. Who suffered? The very people that were in need of help and the very communities that already had more than their fair share of problems. And, " although administered by the Department of Housing and Urban Development rather than OEO, Model Cities reflected the growing appreciation of the urban character of the nation's poor population and was generally perceived as part of the War on Poverty" (ibid.,) But the end result remained the same.

> The vast concrete headquarters of HUD and the Department of Transportation, which occupy adjacent sites of former urban renewal land in the southwest quadrant of Washington, D.C., are monuments to this brief by exuberant era of domestic concern (sadly overshadowed by the other war, in Vietnam) (p. 284).

Finally, it was noted that, "Nationally, more than 1000 local historic preservation laws were in effect as of the mid-1980s" (p. 290). So while there is concern about the aging housing stock and the historical character of the city, there is not an equal amount of concern expressed about the minorities and low-income people who live in many of the areas which have the historic landmark designation!

THE AFRICENTRIC SOCIOURBAN PLANNING PARADIGM: DEFINING DEVELOPMENT IN YOUR OWN IMAGE AND INTERESTS

Poverty pimping, as it has come to be called (at least by me), is big business in major and mid-sized cities. If you can carve out an area that is considered to be low-income, a ghetto or a barrio, then you can get the Federal money year after year without providing ANY evidence of having done anything positive for that area. Of course, if you did, your area would then become so stable that you would no longer qualify for the poverty money. So the key is, as I've written, to keep somebody poor, unemployed and living in substandard housing.

That would be YOU.

Fraser & Kick begin by stating,

> Most recently community building has been framed as anti-poverty work with a heavy component of civil responsibility … **Communities and residents are viewed as ultimately responsible for improving their quality of life in the context of a market economy with increasingly limited state support for social welfare interventions.** This contrasts

> markedly with models of benefits provision for the poor characteristic of earlier decades, and with models of community building that historically have **advocated for the organized resistance of the urban poor against market forces and dominant political-economic and cultural practices that were disadvantaging** (Fraser, & Kick, p. 24 – emphasis added).

Community building was at one time in the hands of grass roots leadership, mainly charismatic people of color, activist whites like Saul Alinsky, and as a result, nonprofit organizations. Those in power saw this trend taking place and sought out to co-opt the movement, and in my view they have been successful. Through the use of grant programs, various "federal projects" and other forms of financial manipulation, those in power have steered community building and re-defined it. Now community building is more about the destruction of housing and planting of urban gardens, programs of neighborhood watching and community festivals than much else. Gone are the days of "save the housing" and marching to organize and inform the grassroots masses.

The previous excerpt claims a decline in approaches that "advocated for the organized resistance of the urban poor against market forces and dominant political-economic and cultural practices that were disadvantaging." This is akin to what I have previously alleged, but it refers to organizers as the urban poor. I view such a term as redundant; to be urban is to be poor because those with money created and have moved into suburbia and exurbia. Only the corporations are on the urban fringe to feed off of what few financial outlets (banks, credit unions) that may be left in the central city.

The fact is, the concept of anti-poverty is not new, but because of some of the social changes that have been implemented since the 1960s when black people decide to light torches and threaten property in order to ratchet up any morals that the system might have, certain wording has been replaced with more palatable terms. Poverty started out meaning low income ethnic white folks (Italians, Poles, Germans, etc.), and then it began to mean "black" for a while.

But now because of the way that the economy has started to gradually slide, the concept of "anti-poverty" has come to mean just that – *anti- low income*. So now white folks are back in that group again, but the disproportionate numbers and percentages of the low-income are still African-American and Latino. Of course there are poor whites: *but they ain't poor because they're white*. Therefore the area left behind is ripe for picking, and that is what the city elites are doing: targeting these areas for "development" so that their developer friends can get paid and the structures built can add more revenue by being rented, leased out, or sold.

The key is to make all of this business appear to be moral and based on a sincere concern for the poor. But the facts are what they are.

Anti-poverty, as viewed by the Africentric Sociourban Planning paradigm, became a matter of civil responsibility because grant writers started putting together proposals for nonprofit corporations who, in turn, decided to enter the anti-poverty game, using the Community Action Agency models of the 1960s. The funding came fast and furiously as, from what I could see, any organization that wanted to "address poverty" had the right to do it – qualified or not. That included churches, community centers, and even human services agencies like the Urban League. The Federal money, during the '60s and '70s, was pouring in.

Grandiose and substanceless names like "Concerted Services" and "Inner City Development Corporation" began springing up. As they did so, you knew a grant of some kind was in the making. They were claiming to be community development programs but were really "economic development outposts." And only a few individuals and families were "getting developed," if you know what I mean.

That is how, gradually, what the authors wrote, came into fruition as they asserted that, "Communities and residents are viewed as ultimately responsible for improving their quality of life in the context of a market economy with increasingly limited state support for social welfare interventions." As I view it, a new paradigm and approach was needed for grass roots people and low-income communities because those in power had successfully co-opted and "bought off" what had taken place earlier.

The reason for the marked shift in models and philosophy was that government listened and heard the words "self-help." It is easier to control people if you make them think that they are taking care of their own issues and problems. This meant that the benefits being provided to the poor had to have strings attached and in fact, those strings would be "pulled" by members of their own groups. In that way, if anyone was to blame, it would be the people who were closest to those who needed the help – not the Federal bureaucracy. There can't be "organized resistance" of the people doing the oppressor look the way you do; at least, that was the way it was in the '60s and '70s. "The man" and "the system" were identified by race and class, not by what was being done to harm you.

Fraser & Kick continue kicking knowledge:

> Data from the U.S. Census Bureau (2002) show that official
> poverty has increased in recent years with 34.6 million people
> now living in poverty. Of this group, nearly 26 million reside
> in metropolitan neighborhoods, with the number of central city
> poverty tracts increasing from 2595 in 1980 to 3221 in the year
> 2000. Residents of urban high poverty tracts were over three

times more likely than those in other city neighborhoods to
receive public assistance, and one and one-half times more
likely to be unemployed. Over 40% of adults in high poverty
urban neighborhoods do not even hold a high school degree
(Fraser & Kick, p. 25).

Of course the previously described information is more than likely even worse now with the economy being worse than it was in 2002. So there is a need for these cities to "hustle grants" to the best of their ability and in order to qualify, they have to make sure that there is a low-income area that they can "target" (even the grant applications themselves refer to these areas as "target markets").

One key to keeping the money coming in is to link education with poverty. That is why when you see negative demographics, you will also see information provided, as is the case in the preceding excerpt, that the people in the area lack high school education, lack a diploma or such and such a percentage has a GED and no college. This is only partially true because when race is interjected into the equation, the concept of education and success is markedly altered. The facts show that white high school dropouts earn more than black high school graduates, white high school graduates earn more than black college graduates, and that when it comes down to experience, white people get hired in many cases, after being trained by a black person who they are then promoted over. This is known as "corporate leapfrogging" and once again it shows how "race," not "space," is the final frontier.

Furthermore, by linking education with poverty you can make money on both ends: the area colleges can increase their enrollments and this is especially true for those proprietary schools that make promises about making students employable and work on a strictly cash economy. These schools do to prospective students what the city does to minority communities: exploit ignorance and create a façade that an education can and will automatically change your life. Rooted in this belief is the oft-held contention that jobs and a higher quality of life are what life is all about and as such, the path to these jobs and higher quality of life is via the educational route. As Giachino (2010) cogently contends,

Education is the path to success and financial stability, but
diploma mills have cheapened that truism, and have been
expensive for students and taxpayers. With Black
unemployment at 16.5 percent and continuing to creep
upward, bulking up educational credentials seems like a good
idea. Especially given that people with lower levels of
education have been pounded even harder in the recession
(Giachino, 2010).

In her seminal study, Chung (2008) investigated whether students self-select into the US for-profit colleges or whether the choice of for-profit sector is accidental or due to the reasons external to the students (geographic exposure to for-profit providers, tuition pricing, or random circumstances). She found that find that students self-select into for-profit sector and found that three groups of "significant factors" stand out: (1) choice of for-profit sector is characterized by lower parental involvement in student's schooling; (2) for-profit-bound students are more likely to display high levels of school absenteeism and to give birth as early as 10th grade; and (3) the average predicted probabilities of choosing for-profit sector increase as in-state public community college tuition rises and county-specific concentration of for-profit providers grows larger (Chung, 2008).

Everybody can make money off the poverty game. You can hunker down and start up a nonprofit to tutor at-risk kids after school even without having any credentials of your own; you can hang out a shingle and offer "affordable legal advise" to the community; you can obtain nonprofit status and then beg for clothes and food which you can then turn around and give out – but only after alerting the media and letting them know the time and place so you can stand there and show everyone how much you love the "negroes." And then, from that public relations coup, you can let the public know that "all donations are tax-deductible."

So all that benevolence that you hear about – the United Way, Catholic Charities, the Salvation Army – they don't do it for free. As nonprofits they continue to get money to hire staff, pay office expenses and also create jobs. They might do good work for the poor, but all this is being done in lieu of providing those same poor with jobs. If they did that, then there would be no need for the poverty pimps, would there?

Ask yourselves: what do we need that is developmental? We know that we need jobs, but in the way that the concept of employment is being defined, it is almost synonymous with finding a white man to adopt you. When we think of "looking for job," our view is always outside of where we live and beyond the realm of our community. How can we be organizers if we are dependent upon the source of our problems to employ us? What happens if we do get hired? How far will we be "allowed" to go? Ever wonder why your leadership is so cautious with their words when they're on television? It's because they know "the boss might we watching" and they don't want to lose their jobs.

When you define development in your own image and interests, you sit down and create a wish list. You know the community and what it needs, and you know that before all these grant programs, social service buildings and other "projects" came into our community, the community not only fared better but it looked better. We got by and the "underground economy" went a long way toward establishing security in our community. We settled our own problems and we didn't have the high rate of homicide that we do today. We can and must do better and it begins by looking internally and then building outward.

KNOW YOUR ENEMY

From time to time you'll see an ad or promo addressing, "The future leaders of tomorrow." In reality, that is redundant. But unbeknownst to the illiterates who make money pawning off such distortions as 'cutting edge appeals,' even a mistake in action can produce, somewhere along the line, something positive. In sum we must operate from a position of power in all decision making. There can be no more paternalistic control of our communities.

A key strategy of those in power to control the community organizers is to change or take control of the lexicon that is used. You will find that your enemy is going to feign a concern for and commitment to the community. Those in power will use terms and phrases like "diversity," "community engagement," and "inclusion" as a way to create a façade of "wanting to help." But as the 1971 song by the group The Undisputed Truth teaches us, also applies to infiltration, community treachery, co-optation and takeover moves by the power structure through pretending to care about the community. The essential lyrics to the song go like this:

Smiling faces sometimes
Pretend to be your friend
Smiling faces show no traces
Of the evil that lurks within

[Chorus]
Smiling faces, smiling faces sometimes
They don't tell the truth
Smiling faces, smiling faces
Tell lies and I got proof

Beware, beware of the handshake
That hides the snake
I'm telling you beware
Beware of the pat on the back
It just might hold you back
I tell you, you can't see behind

Your enemy won't do you no harm
Cause you'll know where he's coming from
Don't let the handshake and the smile fool ya
Take my advice I'm only try' to school ya

"Future leaders of tomorrow," in the context of this book and paradigm (ASP) places the emphasis on the term, "future leaders." What I mean is that they lead the future; they pave the way, define the social realities that, in turn, will lead to a better life for those who need help the most. Without inclusion from grass roots people who live in the communities and neighborhoods most impacted by discrimination, segregation and housing manipulation, the concept of "future leaders" translates to mean "future external controllers."

INTERNAL OPPOSITION: PROVOCATEURS AND RACE-TRAITORS

Over the years, those of us with superior intellect have used that knowledge to create a kind of "hierarchy of consciousness." I'll take the heat although others have also done it: we have wrongly insulted Uncle Tom in our attempts to define those of us who we, as leaders, believe have "sold out" or in some other way, "betrayed" the race.

To begin with, those of you who read the Harriet Beecher Stowe's book, *Uncle Tom's Cabin* (oops! Sorry. I mean those of you who, out of fear of books, saw the movie that starred Avery Brooks). The term was coined after that to mean someone who sold black folks down the river – but why? Uncle Tom, in the end, chose death rather than snitch on the enslaved black folks that had escaped.

But the name refers to his actions: smiling for the master, scratching his head, kowtowing to curry favor, laughing when nothing was funny. This was the behavior that the other enslaved folks looked at with disdain and behavior that would later be emulated by the likes of Mantan Moreland, Stepin Fetchin and to a lesse extent, "Rochester" Anderson. But in the latter case, it was for laughs and the appeasement of Anglos.

"Tomming" was a survival tactic. But here is what no one wants to write or talk about as it relates to the education of our future leaders: I have found that there is a direct correlation between the amount tomming you have to do and the amount of ability and intelligence that you have. Put simply, if you're a moron, then you have to tom a lot in order to get in, get ahead or, as we used to say, "get over." But if you have ability, and you have some semblance of consciousness, you can put yourself in a position where you can not only survive, but also do so with some semblance of dignity while at the same time caring for your families.

Case in point: black women. Now although the term for them is "Aunt Jemima" (who never sold out anyone but was a creation of some pancake people), it is clear that over the years they have played a major role in the survival of black people. During that time they have had to endure untold horrors of working for Anglos in their homes, serving as nannies and the like. They had to smile, laugh and listen to others poke fun at sometimes even watch as Anglos harmed or killed black people. From slavery to the present, this has been the case.

Does that make them "toms"? No. But what they did was in the way of survival. What we have to look at is just how important is what we do to the end result of caring for those we care about? Young leaders have to get other people of color to ask, "is this tommin' necessary"?

Those of us who have our own businesses or intellectual ability have to worry about this less. But in my case (others can pretend they never did it) I have used that term far too often to describe black folks who were simply trying to eke out an existence. Did they betray the race? Did they humiliate black folks? No. And here's why: these kinds of folks are not the exception – they are the RULE!

That's right, I said it: black people, in general, are "toms." I used to get phone calls from people telling me that Senator Chambers was wrong for calling black people Uncle Toms. But I agree with Ernie: look at what we've produced as a race. That is how you judge a group: what do they, as a collective, produce that, in turn, can help them with their own growth and development? When you ask that question you come to a very simple answer: *nada.*

Don't get me wrong, we built this country and we've made others great. But those strong and smart enough to bake the pie should be astute enough to see that once the pie is finished, they deserve at least a slice of it! Our people have "tommed" and, at one time, it may have been a survival tactic. But today, in 21st century America we do it for one reason and one reason alone: because its comfortable and it feels good.

We have gotten away with doing nothing for so long that when somebody does something, we take offense to it. Like our former slavemasters, we look at that person with disdain-and-how-dare-you and work to isolate ourselves from him or her. You've seen it before. The same people that smile in your face and say "good job" when outsiders aren't looking are the same ones that are running back and currying favor, joining their bosses in "dealing with those militants" and those "rabble-rousers."

Tomming is not unique to us. White folks (the original toms) have it down to a science, especially in corporate America. They call it, "brown nosing." I've seen it, and it is hilarious. What is funny is that those who do it share the same fate as the blacks who do: those in power, because of the 1960s and the consciousness that we ushered into existence, know when someone is tomming! It used to fool them; now, for the most part, it no longer does.

So what's the purpose?

If we don't need it in order to survive, then why do it? Furthermore, if we do need to do it in order to survive, maybe we're in the wrong business. Maybe if you have to tom to get a good grade or a degree, or if you have to tom to keep your job or get that promotion, maybe you don't deserve any of it. Maybe all those black people laid their lives down or put those lives on the line so that future generations wouldn't HAVE to tom any more. The early toms knew how degrading the act was, but in the name of future generations, did it so that we wouldn't have to. Feel me?

Understanding now that denunciation rarely leads to definition, I share my information with young folks. Of course I still "dog" people that I think aren't doing what they should be. But just write it off as a personality quirk of mine, but a political necessity for future leaders.

One last thing: you can create more etymologically correct terms whenever and wherever you choose. Rather than using either "Uncle Tom" or "Aunt Jemima," I created the term "Gungamima." Gunga Din was a man in India who sold out his people to the British and when he died, they paid him the ultimate compliment by saying that he had, "a white heart." His betrayal led to the slaughters of tens of thousands of his people. So we take his first name ("Gunga") and add to it that ending of "Jemima," and we come up with a gender-neutral term to be used to those, male or female, who act in a way that embarrasses, humiliates or in some other way harms black folks. "Gungamima."

So remember: if you've got skills, tomming is less of a necessity. In 21st century America, we need to look inward because we have communities that dominate most cities and with numbers usually comes power. The fact that we are still lagging in the power category clearly shows that in the final analysis, tommin' don't work.

Leaders of the future, this is important information. Our numbers are too small to be throwing anybody away. Those that will leave will do so on their own. In the meantime, it is up to us to close ranks, educate ourselves and remember the words of George Jackson: "Every sickness ain't death, every good-bye ain't gone, and every big man ain't strong."

EXTERNAL OPPOSITION: READ AND STUDY THE WORDS OF ELITES

The elites are the people that run Omaha; some of them are elected and others are not. The ones with the money control the ones who have political office, but the ones in political office are the ones who tend to commit their plans, views and values onto paper. And this is what you must study and read in order to have the keys to real empowerment.

As a case in point I now share with you an analysis of a a 2004 speech by former Mayor Mike Fahey. Study well and you will see how men of his ilk distort the truth, boast of what "will be," and tend to ignore issues of race and class.

In a word, for a long time, the City of Omaha has been playing cosmetic games with Federal money while the urban core suffers because of the lack of essential infrastructure repairs, jobs and job development, and relevant social services. This cannot be seen more plainly than when one reads the words of current mayor Mike Fahey, the most recent in a long line of city leaders who have ignored the infrastructure needs of Omaha while concentrating on downtown, the far west, the southwest and mid town areas of the city.

CASE STUDY
The Geo-Politics of Community Growth: Mayor Mike
Fahey's January 2004, "State of the City Address"

Two things can be gleaned from Mayor Mike Fahey's "State of the City Address," delivered in January of 2004. The first thing is that like former University of Nebraska at Omaha Chancellor Del Weber, he is a "bricks and mortar" man. Weber, during his decades as the leader of the city's largest university, flopped in the area of human relations, but was able to spearhead the construction of buildings all over campus. That then, was his legacy: bricks and mortar over bodies and morality. The same can be said for Mayor Mike Fahey, as you will see in the following speech.

Secondly, as a result of the first character flaw, Fahey's own words make it clear that what is being done to other parts of the city of Omaha is not being done in the area where the most help is needed. Following are excerpts from Mayor Mike Fahey's January 5, 2004 "State of the City Address."

The Mayor begins:

> In Omaha's early days, life centered on the Missouri River. However, as we grew west, north and south over the years the river became less important. But 2003 marked a significant change when Omaha returned to its roots to build a prosperous modern future. And national media – from outlets like the New York Times. Washington Post, Chicago Tribune and Kansas City Star – are not only writing about Omaha's recent success, but one actually called on their local government leaders to look at Omaha as a model for downtown renewal.

Fahey begins by claiming that life began on the Missouri River, and as can be expected, links Omaha's early nexus to that which is geographic. But the fact of the matter is that is not the case. Omaha's early beginning centered on relocating American Indians following the incursions of white military officers who invaded this area and slaughtered countless tens of thousands of natives. This is how Omaha started: conceived in violence and dedicated to the proposition that all white men are created equal.

He claims that as the city grew, the river became less important. That again, is a geographic statement because the mayor, in speaking for his fellow whites, shows that the river area – which includes the black community – was neglected. His claim of "growth" to the west, north and south omits the manner in which that growth takes place. And he also forgets to mention that the "we" and the "our" is in reference to white folks. They expanded and then in the 1960s, ran from black folks, and created their own communities. You can not "forget" about the river and not also forget about the people who live nearest to it: black folks and low-income whites. If Omaha was located in the South, this area of the city that Fahey is talking about would be called "the bottoms."

One thing about these racist mayors that Omaha elects to office is that they all try to make that life is mute until they come along and take care of what should have been taken care of all along. In Fahey's case, 2003 supposedly "marks a significant change." For whom? His white business buddies and his political cronies, that's who. Fahey opened the gates for business encroachment and the continued abuse of federal block grant money, continuing the legacy and method of operation established by former Mayor Hal Daub.

Fahey talks of Omaha "returning to its roots." This is a racist statement, because Omaha's roots are the roots of people who love the water, but they don't love the people who live near it. To make such a claim makes it appear as if white folks returned to the east side. That is a lie. They come back to the area for freakishness and frolic, for leisure and drunken pleasure. Then they return to their western suburban homes. Like Fahey, these white people want nothing to do with any area of the city that is close to the black community. They will party there and socialize there, but only because they know they won't be there long. Most Omahans share the racial mentality and sophistication of whites in the Deep South during the 1920s.

Fahey's examples of success are geographic and architectural. He knows that he can boast of no level of sophistication on the part of his white cohorts, because they are the racists who maintain black subjugation. When Fahey talks about the national media and the coverage of Omaha, he has to qualify the statement with the fact that these media are looking "at Omaha as a model for downtown renewal."

First of all, that is a lie. Omaha steals its ideas from Kansas City and Denver. There is nothing unique about what is going on downtown because the people in the planning department are white boys who couldn't cut it in any other city. One of the former members didn't even have a college degree and was a manic depressive on meds making decisions that involved millions of dollars. *Omaha does its city planning based on racist whim and business objectives;* there is little concern for providing jobs and even less concern about working WITH people of color. It seems that all the city administration knows is IMPOSITION.

So he brags about downtown and its buildings because there is nothing he can say about culture or race relations because Omaha scores a big fat zero in those areas; imagine, a hick town with no gas stations downtown, no night life and whose businesses shut down at 9:00 at night!

Fahey's fabricated fantasies continue has he continues his foray into the world of "bricks and mortar:"

> Together, we cleared away an overgrown, littered riverfront and created a new and welcoming gateway to our city. Abbott Drive and 10th Street now boast new perspectives on downtown Omaha's blossoming cityscape and connect the airport to our main business district to some of our world-class attractions such as the zoo and Laurentzen (sic) Gardens. Gallup University opened our business and so did the Qwest Center Omaha, Union Pacific's new headquarters continues to take shape and joins First National Bank's tower in our skyline. While brand new, it's already hard to imagine our city without them.

Fahey has selective memory. That "overgrown, littered riverfront" was cleared away until those white people saw that other cities were making money from THEIR riverfronts. For so long, that riverfront was considered a part of the ghetto, and was used as nothing more than a dumping ground for some of Fahey's white corporate friends.

Fahey talks about the "gateway to our city." That Gateway, as he calls it, tears right through North Omaha if you head north from the airport. That Gateway, as he calls it, used black poverty-generated CDBG funds to make way for expanding Abbott Drive. That Gateway, and its Pearl of Lights cost more than this mayor has spent on sidewalks, lights or sewers in the black community, which is less than three miles away from that "gateway." What they've done is build AROUND North Omaha while all the while using the Federal funds that black poverty generated.

Fahey talks about connecting the airport to their main business district. It is not their main business district. What he means is "central business district." The main business district is no longer downtown; it is west, and well he should know. He talks of world class attractions like the (Henry Doorly) zoo and the Lauritzen Gardens. This proves that while he is willing to spend money on those attractions that are already stable, he is intentionally abandoning the deteriorating area that is a few scant miles from his City Hall offices. If this isn't the "triage approach," then show me what is.

Like his predecessor Daub, he seems more concerned about the city's skyline than he is about the area just north of where that skyline is located. Fahey has done nothing in or for the black community, and yet this is the community that ushered him into office (he only beat Daub by 700-odd votes). And he repays us by appointing black Uncle Toms (Chris Rodgers, Reginald Young, and Gail Thompson, to name but a few) and doling out some chump-change grants for neighborhood projects.

He had the nerve to say, in regard to the National Bank Tower, the Qwest Center and the new Union Pacific Headquarters that, "while brand new, it's already hard to imagine our city without them." Buildings. Concrete. Steel beams. Glass. This is what this white man is about. He wants to leave a legacy of architecture just as Daub did. But when it comes to the concerns of the black community, he is so beholden to the business community that even if he wanted to do something, he couldn't. After all, the white business owners and their corporate counterparts are in bed with the City of Omaha, Creighton University and the University of Nebraska-Omaha in the encroachment upon North Omaha. They write grants documenting black poverty, then spend the money on their "whites-only" programs and projects. THIS then, is the Fahey legacy.

He continues with his geopolitical and architectural descriptions of is "vision:"

> Soon the Hilton Omaha will open its doors to convention goers and secure its place as our city's flagship hotel. The Missouri River Pedestrian Bridge will span the river redefining Omaha again, and will be the first pedestrian bridge in the nation to link two states. Riverfront Place will introduce Omahans to a brand new kind of urban living with high-rise condominiums and town homes with a spectacular view of downtown and the river.

The Omaha Hilton was built despite a controversy that included Council member arguing about whether or not it was the best one to choose from. But since it was built, the local media has joined in with covering up the realities of the building, including a recent news report by WOWT-Channel 6. During that report, it was announced that the Hilton had just received "a four diamond rating" and the report made it appear as if this was the top award that existed. After checking, I found out that, just like the "star' rating system, "four diamond is not top of the line – five diamond is.

So the Hilton is not a top rated hotel, but since Fahey has claimed it is the city's flagship hotel, it is clear that once again, Omaha shows that it is accustomed to glorifying its mediocrity, in much the same way that it covers up the racist employment policies of its new buildings: few blacks working at the World Herald's Freedom Center, the Qwest Center, the Union Pacific headquarters or the First National Bank Tower (except as janitors and cooks, just like it was in the 1940s).

The Missouri Valley Pedestrian Bridge was no major deal, and while wihte folks can boast that it is the only bridge in the nation to link two states, that is probably because other states are above such trivial and foolish "firsts." Perhaps other states are working to spend money on its low-income communities, and not on silly walkways to appease suburban white folks who don't live anywhere near where the bridge was built. This is the kind of crap that Fahey boasts about while covering up the long-time neglect of the state of Nebraska's largest African-American community.

Then it's back to the river again as he talks about the construction of Riverfront Place, which he claims will usher in a "new kind of urban living with high rise condos and town homes." See how these silly white men think? They don't have the size to be considered an urban city, but they want to pretend that they are. Cursed with backward thinking hicks and political hacks who gamble, take bribes and switch parties on a whim, Omaha is a joke across much of the country. Fahey, like other uninformed white folks, think that "urban" can be defined by the housing stock. He thinks that condos and town homes will give these hicks some kind of urban sophistication. But he is wrong. The racist and countrified attitude that these white folks have will forever consign them to a category of hillbillies. And all the condominiums and all the annexations in the world won't change that.

Finally, note where Fahey speaks about the "spectacular view of downtown and the river." This was what it was all about all the time. These white people, cowards who fled the area when black people started moving into the area, now want to return to the area. They want that view and they want access to the river, but more importantly than all that, they tire of the long commute from downtown (where there are supposedly 25,000 jobs) to the suburbs. These people want to return and have access to the lovely boulevards and flat land that North Omaha has more than enough of. They want proximity to the airport (although the North Freeway, which was built through the heart of the black community, was built to accommodate them so they could get from their suburban homes to Eppley Airfield). So even as they crave the "return to the riverfront" (which is, by the way, their slogan), they are also engaged in a strategy to relocate as many black people as they can to the urban fringe.

The Mayor's address continues:

> Our task now is to build upon the great momentum generated
> by riverfront work. Like our public private partnerships, we
> must refocus then drive and ambition that rebuilt the
> Missouri Riverfront, capture its energy and push it into our
> neighborhoods and smaller business districts. We're doing
> just that with successful neighborhood programs and focused
> economic development plans. Omaha's neighborhood remain
> a priority and great work is happening throughout the city
> through tour Neighborhood Grant Program, our residential
> street resurfacing program and the Neighborhood Parks and
> Libraries Renovation Plan.

More about the Riverfront – but nothing about the people who live closest to it who they have ROBBED of millions of dollars in Community Development Block Grant funds since 1975. And even before that, they abused and pocketed and benefited from urban renewal monies, Model Cities funds as well as Urban Development Action Grants, Small Neighborhood Action program grants, and today its Community Service Block Grants, Weed and Seed Funds, Project Safe Neighborhoods and other monies that do more to employ white folks than to assist the low income. The Riverfront is one more way for these people to build for the sake of fun, frolic and leisure at the expense of those holed up in the black community.

Fahey uses code words like "private partnerships," and "focused economic development" as ways to explain how these greedy white people monopolize all the money, build and demolish at a whim, are able to receive the backing of banks and other lenders without a whim, and yet, even amid all this, they still despise black people so much that once a project is built on the eastern fringe of the black community (that is where the "riverfront" is), these racists won't even hire any.

The duplicitous Fahey boasts about his Neighborhood Parks and Libraries Renovation Plan, and yet when it came to the library that serves the black community – the Charles Washington Library – there was no real "plan" on what to do with the books while the building was being remodeled. A last minute idea meant that blacks would be going to the nearby Benson Library, a library that had been modeled long ago even though it served fewer people than the Washington Library did. The black community is once again coming last for services: last to get cable TV hookups, last to get caller identification and other phone services, last to get its library repaired. Fahey didn't start this tradition; he simply perpetuated it.

From there, he stoops to outright lying. Check it out:

> We awarded 40 grants to neighborhood associations in the
> past two years. While these grants are relatively small -
> $5,000 or less – they've made a tremendous impact on our
> city's neighborhood communities. From banners to
> landscaping, from signage to safety lighting many areas of
> Omaha re visibly improved. I hope to be able to expand both
> the size and number of grants in the future.

When Fahey says that the grants are "$5,000 or less," he is being generous. In 2002, when Fahey awarded the first of the Neighborhood Improvement Grants, he only set aside $85,000 from the general fund. Of the twenty four Omaha neighborhoods that received grants in 2002, only ten of them were North of Dodge Street (the black community and its fringe). Those groups were Belvedere Point Neighborhood ($5,000), Bemis Park Neighborhood ($5,000), Benson Neighborhood ($3,505), Central Park ($1,500), Conestoga Place Homeowners ($1,500), Dundee Memorial ($2,500), Dundee Neighborhood (*$2,500), Florence Futures Neighborhood ($4,240), Gifford Park ($3,065), Miller Park-Minne Lusa ($1,800). (Omaha Star, 2002: 1).

These ten neighborhoods, either in or close to the black community, have a total of $30,550. This averages out to just over $3,000 per organization. But with the other 14 groups who were awarded sharing a combined total of just under $55,000, we can see where Fahey's interests are. Not with the poor neighborhoods with zip codes like 68111, 68110 or 68104, but on the midtown and white areas. In fact, even of those north of Dodge, perhaps the most racist of the neighborhood groups, Dundee, received two separate grants, one under "Dundee Memorial" and the other under "Dundee Neighborhood." Furthermore, Florence Futures, Bemis Park and Miller Park have some blacks, but these are mainly white focused neighborhood groups.

These facts send a direct message to black folks regarding Fahey's "vision." As he said in August of 2002, "I am proud of this program and look forward to the results" (Omaha Star, 2002: 1).

Furthermore, there was no "tremendous impact" made on any neighborhoods that are located in the black community. That chump change that was doled out came from black people's money in the first place! Fahey is afraid of change because, as most people know, he's afraid of the black community. He had no plan on what to do when he got elected. He realized that black people were the ones who put him over the top, but he had to phone up several community leaders to ask who he should appoint! That shows that when it comes to black people, this man had no vision. The fact remains simple: black people voted AGAINST former Mayor Hal Daub, not FOR Mike Fahey! But he's shown what he thinks of black people by letting the police run rampant over the black community, by continuing to allow the abuse of CDBG funds, and by the way he's allowing Workforce Development to be watered down so that the white folks being laid off Countywide can get priority services over minority applicants and clients.

During his address, he claimed that,

> ... the program has sparked ingenuity as many neighbors
> are now working together and building long-term plans for
> their neighborhoods. That's exactly what these grants were
> supposed to do - promote new plans, vision and growth,
> that is largely driven by the people who live there. I am
> proud I initiated this important neighborhood program and
> look forward to its continued success.

How can you "spark ingenuity" when ingenuity is the power of creative imagination? What is creative about what these white people are doing? In their own way, what they are doing is maintaining the segregated condition of the city. The neighborhoods that deserve the lion's share of the money – those located in the black community – are not getting any money and those that do are not getting the maximum amount. So why is Fahey lying?

The only neighborhood association that presented a real "plan" was the Triple One Neighborhood Association. This was a plan that was communitywide, would have created over 200 jobs, and would have empowered the area. Instead, he opted to provide funds for neighborhood watch groups, planting a few shrubs and other trivial activities. This is his version of "vision and growth."

Fahey has not mentioned human beings one time in his speech. Therefore the allegation about him being about "bricks and mortar" continues to hold – just as it does in the following series of statements:

> Because we blended new technology with old methods, our
> residential street resurfacing program continues to pave
> more streets than ever. This year 152 blocks were resurfaced
> and 35 were rebuilt in our residential areas; forth-three lane
> miles in our major streets program were paved. Two years
> ago, I crated the Neighborhood Parks and Libraries
> Renovation Plan to renovate 70 neighborhood parks and 5
> libraries across the city that otherwise would have taken 15
> to 20 years to complete.

Fahey boasts about a road resurfacing program that in reality, for the past two decades, has been nothing more than an overtime moneymaker for the lily-white Department of Public Works as well as some white sub contractors. Ask any one around Omaha: damn near every summer, during the height of tourist season, these white folks are out paving the roads. Evidently, they're not doing a very good job because the asphalt they put down and the way that they do it doesn't last very long; the following year, there they are again, blocking off key streets and paving the same streets over and over again. No one says anything to them about it, but you can hear people complaining all over the city.

So when you hear this man talk about 152 blocks being "resurfaced," he doesn't mention that most of those blocks were just "resurfaced" last year! He then begins bragging about the parks that were renovated, but doesn't mention the fact that the parks were in disrepair for almost two years while he was in office. His "better-late-that-never" approach hurt the parks in the black community the most, especially Miami Park, and smaller parks in the neighborhood. Like his predecessor, Hal Daub, he never asked the residents of the areas what they felt the parks needed the most. Daub had already ruined Miller Park because he had a chance to put a major sized swimming pool there but instead, spent hundreds of thousands on a wading pool! The point here is that this "State of the City speech" seems to be about construction, repairs and expansion – different sides of the "bricks and mortar" orientation and emphasis.

With 2004 being an election year, it would figure that a man running for Mayor would make promises about improving parks in the white part of the city and the suburbs; or, as he put it,

> This coming summer four Omaha neighborhood parks, including Sunnyslope, Roanoake, Fillmore and Lee Valley Parks, open again boasting new equipment, trails and/ or green spaces. Another nine will open nest fall. Planning meetings for another 12 parks are scheduled this year. It's fabulous news for families and Omaha's neighborhood and this work will continue on schedule.

When Fahey talks about "Omaha's families," he is not talking about the black or Latino families. He, like other whites who think that their values and views are representative of everyone (as in, "everyone loved and will Miss the late president Ronald Reagan"), is talking about what white folks white and will enjoy. His entire administration clearly showed that when it came to black folks, this man was even more naïve and non-productive than the man many consider to be Omaha's most racist mayor, Hal Daub.

All this talk about the white areas of town and what he plans to do for the physical plant and then he comes to North Omaha. And as he talks about the North and South areas of the city, he moves from tangible and productive business and development to his plans to turn the minority areas of the city into "freak show tourist areas" for white entertainment and consumption. In Fahey's words,

<blockquote>
Unique economic development plans for many areas of
Omaha are aggressively moving forward. The North and
South 24 Street Corridors are well on the way to becoming
destinations. New business and social outlets will build upon
each area's rich history and entice Omahans to the area with
entertainment and business opportunities. These new
destinations can and will join our successful Old Market as
tourist and destination spots.
</blockquote>

Black folks in Omaha just can't catch a break. Instead of applying the regular, traditional economic plans that have worked in other parts of the city, what does this white man talk about? Fahey refers to them as, "unique economic development plans" and claims that these plans are "aggressively moving forward." First of all, the very fact that anything is being done at all is what makes the plans "unique." Secondly, the economic development plans that Fahey is talking about is transforming the black community into a place where middle-class and upper class white folks can frolic and play around. The core of the area, 24th and Lake Street, is even now being turned into what Fahey calls "a cultural arts district" and once again, in Harlem Renaissance-type fashion, the black community gets art, music and dance while the white folks get money, asset accumulation and economic growth.

Even Fahey refers to them as "destination spots." Why? Because the black community is contiguous and adjacent to the Qwest Center and, as importantly, Creighton is in cahoots with the City in encroaching upon North Omaha. You can also add Boys Town and Mutual of Omaha to the mix. Blacks will slowly be concentrated further to the northwest while white folks cordon off the Riverfront with housing (and police and security forces) and gated communities. North Omaha will remain poor because that is the poverty that attracts the Federal funds needed that enables the City, in turn, to use the money making life more appealing to white people whose racism perpetuates the poverty in the first place!

One or two lines about North Omaha (the ghetto) and South Omaha (the barrio) and then its own to another part of the city, one with white businesses and corporations (Mutual of Omaha, Clarkson Hospital, huge Salvation Army corporate sites, Commercial Federal savings, three television stations (KETV-Channel 7, WOWT-Channel 6 and KPTM-Channel 42). It's called "Destination Midtown," and look how it is described:

<blockquote>
An unprecedented effort was launched last year to better
define future development in Omaha's midtown. Named
Destination Midtown, it's a team of leaders representing
</blockquote>

small and big business, neighborhoods, education and city
government. The long-term goal is a complete renovation of
the midtown area, which will dramatically improve the
residential and business environment of an important part of
our city. These recommendations will be presented this
spring and I am excited to see them.

The fact that the effort aimed at midtown was "unprecedented" is yet another testimonial to the ass backwards planning of Omaha's city administration. In most cities, the central business district is the hub, and then, using a concentric type strategy (like the rings on a target), you develop outward. Were that the case in Omaha, midtown would have had second ranking right behind the downtown business district and North Omaha. But being the racists that they are, and being suburbanites themselves, the planners have avoided downtown (except for huge buildings to shape their skyline), skipped over Omaha, the near Northside and the near Southside, and shot all the way out to the western part of the city, annexing more chunks of surrounding areas to increase their population and, in doing so, stretching out limited city services. But these people are about money: the larger the population, the more money you get from the Federal government. So they go out west and add more white folks to the city's taxpayer rolls, over-extend city services to appease the newcomers, and avoid North Omaha altogether.

Fahey often talks about "leaders" and in this case, "teams of leaders." But don't be fooled; what he really means are "business leaders," which is the group he is most beholden to. When it comes to blacks however, he picks out novices and sellouts who know nothing about the black community and who, for the most part, don't live in it. He can't define leadership in any other way but in terms of business because that's all he's about: a middle-aged millionaire with no previous political credentials. And that is what he picks when it comes to these committees and "teams." What Fahey shows is the validity of the adage that, "you can't teach what you don't know, and you can't lead where you won't go."

Just as this white man can predict, anticipate, project and foresee the "goal" of "the complete renovation of the midtown area," he could have done the same thing with North Omaha, if he had the will. But remember the triage approach; write North Omaha off as dying or dead, and then use the resources for areas that area already stable. Furthermore, the more North Omaha deteriorates, the more Federal funds you can apply for and once those funds arrive, spend then every else BUT North Omaha. That ensures continual infusions of new money for the rest of the city and also ensures the gradual decline of the black community. And a financially deteriorated area of any community is an area that is easy to relocate. The "pocket of poverty" that is needed to qualify for federal funds therefore moves from one area of the ghetto to another. Re-segregation.

Fahey knows what he's doing in terms of neglecting North Omaha. His own words prove it in the following excerpt:

> Omaha has successful business districts, from Benson to
> Millard, Florence to Keystone and Dundee and many more.
> These small districts are economic engines for neighborhood
> communities and strengthen the fabric of the whole
> community. City support continues to help these
> communities thrive and I intend to continue my efforts to do
> all that is possible.

Look at the areas that Fahey rightfully notes as "successful business districts." None of them in North Omaha. In fact, when low-income housing was supposed to be placed in the Keystone area, those white folks turned out in droves to resist it and got the City Council to continually 'revise' the plan and then STILL found it unacceptable. Their visions of "hordes of Negroes" coming into their lily-white area is at the root of their resistance, but they lie and claim that it's a matter of population density. In many cases these are the same white folks that lived in communes during the 1960s and you don't get much more "dense" than that! But of course, their true concerns are racial in nature, Fahey knows it, but does nothing to address it. His laissez-faire approach aids and abets these racists in their segregationist tendencies. As he put it, "City support continues to help these communities thrive" and thrive they shall – with as few blacks involved as possible

These white mayors want to re-name the black community so as not to remind themselves of THEIR role in the historical neglect that has been a triage approach to community development. For instance, look at how Fahey describes the area:.

> The renovation of the North Downtown area is also under
> way., Nestled between the Missouri Riverfront, Downtown
> Omaha and Creighton University, the area's fantastic
> development potential is clear and will again be shaped with
> key community input. This part of North Omaha has long
> been neglected and now has an outstanding and exciting
> future.

The "North Downtown area"? What is that? Based on the way that white folks are encroaching on the area, they are talking about as far north as Cuming. This is where Creighton University establishes the northern boundary. Of course, they are encroaching into the urban core, but they do not want to consider that as a part of downtown, although the black community is contiguous to this area.

The fact is, by calling it "North downtown," Fahey is showing how racist he and his planning department really are. They want to designate that they are not going to include North Omaha as part of the plans for the future; they are not going to include North Omaha as part of the plans for development. While linking Creighton University to their plans, even the ignorant Fahey has to acknowledge that, "This part of North Omaha has long been neglected and now has an outstanding and exciting future." Why? Because the white man has decided to seize control of that future.

By undermining, under-funding, rejecting and stealing black-initiated paradigms and proposals for community development, the white man now comes in with his plans, plans that do not include the areas residents. He builds in the area, but has no blacks on the construction teams; he plans for the area but includes no blacks that live in the area or have background in urban planning; he develops in the area but only consults those blacks who have money as their primary motive, rather than the long-term well-being of the black community. And it is taking place and the black community's residents remain as poor as they were back in 1975 when the city of Omaha first received Community Development Block Grants. There is only one reason why this could be the case in the face of more than $140 million in CDBG funds received and all the promises made: *black community deterioration and residential degradation is by design.*

Lies containing the words "exciting future," "bright future," "bright horizon" and the like have been uttered before and are well documented, When it comes to the neglect and denial of North Omaha and its citizenry, the game remains the same even while the players themselves may change. In the final analysis, the overview and supervision of any project or paradigm will be linked to ways to empower and enrich white folks. As Mayor Fahey put it,

> And all these economic development plans and studies will be
> tied together in a new citywide initiative regarding the future
> development of our community called Omaha By Design.
> Another unique collaboration between our public and private
> sectors.

The key words of their silly phrase is "by design." It is "by design" that black people remain segregated. It is "by design" that black people are the most unemployed segment of the economy. It is "by design" that the black infant mortality rate is three times what it is for whites. It is "by design" that these people have stolen more than $140 million in Community Development Block Grant money from North Omaha since 1975. And as you can see, Fahey admits it. This is the Omaha they want, the Omaha they're looking to improve, and the

Omaha that in no way includes black people – other than as a class to be exploited and jailed. The proof is in the pudding.

And in this "design," where black people are so blatantly abused, the City is involved in what could be called "partners in paternalism." Included in that group are Creighton University, the University of Nebraska at Omaha, Metropolitan Community College, Mutual of Omaha, The Omaha World Herald, Union Pacific, the Douglas County Board, Shukert and Associates and a number of others. All of these rich white people make money while the area to be divided up and encroached upon – North Omaha – remains poor and too weak to do anything but wander.

If a single name is to be mentioned in a speech by a racist mayor, it will be the name of someone who is doing the system's bidding. Take note of the following passage from the Mayor's ethnocentric speech:

> Public safety offered our city some of it's highest and lowest moments. The death of Sgt. Jason Tye Pratt was Omaha's darkest day. It is the coldest reality of police work and his loss is truly beyond words. His tragic and senseless death challenges all of us to honor his life by keeping the promise he made – to work hard every day to make or city a better place to live.

In the preceding statement what you find are outright lies. And that is what these white people do; they pawn off glittering generalities as universal facts. You've heard them do it time and time again, claiming that what THEY believe is what EVERYBODY believes. In this particular case, it's Tye Pratt, the white cop that was chasing down a black suspect and then got killed as a result. And the entire city went mad! They had regular programming pre-empted on four networks, they held the funeral in a major auditorium and they marched his blonde, trophy wife out to cry out against a judicial system that put the shooter (Albert Rucker) on the streets. But they held back some information.

One thing they held back was the reason why Rucker, an habitual criminal, was out on the streets was because the Omaha Police Department was using him as a snitch. There is no telling how many black folks went to jail because of information provided by Rucker. Evidently, Rucker – as do many confidential informants – felt that he was above the law. He wasn't. Tye Pratt's fellow officer, last name Pratt, capped Rucker and killed him.

Fahey praises this one officer and says that his death bought low moments for the entire city. Aren't blacks part of the city? All the death bought black people was more evidence of how cowardly Fahey was in confronting the issues that followed. Here, in a nutshell is what took place.

After Pratt was killed, a black minister named Bishop William Barlowe donated $100 to Pratt's two young children in the name of Rucker's children. A television show host, who is also a well-known black police officer, Tariq Al-Amin, didn't appreciate the gesture. His position was that Barlowe had no right to donate money in the name of Rucker's children, as if those children had something to do with it or as if their father was somehow in the wrong. Al-Amin, during one of his shows, held up a straight razor and said he was donating it to the Rucker children so that when they grew up, they could cut Barlowe's throat for making such a degrading donation.

Al-Amin was first, suspended for a short time and then a black police chief, Tommy Warren, was hired. Warren's first order of business? To terminate Al-Amin from the department. Al-Amin appealed and then with a wealth of community support, was able to win back his job. Fahey was nowhere to be found during this incident and had nothing to say. When asked about the controversy, Fahey said it was a matter for the City's Personnel Department. This is how "hands on" he is when it comes to dealing with racial issues – but he invokes the name of Tye Pratt so that he can curry favor with the police department.

Even his reference to "Omaha's darkest day" says a lot about Fahey. First of all, the shooting one one cop is not enough to make it the worst day for any city as large as Omaha. But secondly, if it was, why does the day have to be designated as being "dark"? Why do these white people, who lie to their children and say that racism is over, continue to use words like "dark" and "black" to describe all that is negative, hurtful, dirty or evil? It's called "meta-racism" and Kovel (1970) defines it as racism that goes beyond the every day overt acts, but indeed, people can be devoid of racial prejudice but because they acquiesce in the larger cultural order, they are unconsciously racist rather they know it or not. This is Fahey's problem: he thinks that appointing unqualified "negroes" to lead key departments is not a racist act because the participants are black. But he intentionally appoints those he knows are not qualified hoping that in doing the bidding for whites, these "negroes" will also ignore and insult the black community.

Fahey's whole approach has been one of meta-racism; the friendly smile even as he appoints a police chief who has black skin, but an apparent utter contempt for black people. Talking about neighborhood development even as he perpetuates the racist tradition against North Omaha. Claiming to want to restore unity to city hall while allowing the police department to conduct illegal DNA searches on black men in North Omaha, with vague descriptions, in the name of a search for an alleged "serial rapist." This is the test to Fahey's character. And on Triple One's report card, this mayor comes in with a "D-minus."

First, check out what he has to say about the fire chief and his appointments to the Fire Department:

> Now, new chiefs in both the Omaha Police and Fire
> departments have set a course that will position our public
> safety teams for professional community-driven leadership
> well into the future. Chief Robert Dahlquist and Assistant
> Chiefs Jim Love, Mark Rohlfing, and Jack York reflect the
> rich traditions that Omahans expect from leaders – including
> public service, leadership, education, family and a love for
> our city and its citizens. Not surprisingly, Chief Dahlquist
> comes from a family of public servants. His late father,
> Horton, also served as fire chief.

These white firemen are not less racist than their ancestors. Fahey, by his own admission, appoints one because of a "family tradition." But in his ignorance he cannot see that as far as black people are concerned, the hiring and appointment policies of whites all over Omaha is based on a "family tradition;" a tradition that makes it clear that there black folks need not apply. The appointment of cops also shows Fahey's meta-racism, pure and simple:

> Police Chief Thomas Warren is a native Omahan and deeply
> committed to public serve and community policing. Eric
> Buske and Don Thorson, whom I promoted to Deputy Police
> Chief, join him as OPD's new leadership team. To name
> three top managers at once was a unique opportunity, but was
> also an obvious choice. All three could have been police
> chief most anywhere in the country. It made sense to put
> them all in leadership positions, and I am pleased I had the
> opportunity to do so. Omaha will be better for their efforts.

In this case, a black man, with more than 20 years experience on the workforce, scored higher than anyone on the police tests, and was the leading finisher among the top three candidates. But Fahey and others know how fickle the white man is and they know how racist the city is. So they could not appoint a black man as police chief without also doing "something" for the two white boys would couldn't cut it. So that is what Fahey did: he promoted all three of them. This was a move that downplayed the accomplishment by the black appointee, who was to become the first black police chief in Omaha history.

Fahey needed someone to make the termination of police officer Tariq Al-Amin permanent, because if a white man did it it would look like racism. So he selected Warren. Even though Warren had the best marks, this doesn't mean anything in Omaha, where more than a few black men violated laws of protocol to stop from being seen as "nigger lovers." Secondly, Warren was making history and

Fahey would be able to tell the black community that Warren was a minority. White folks, for the most part, appreciate, but can't quite figure what an Uncle Tom is. Fahey thinks that appointing Warren is going to curry favor with black voters. But Warren's recent speech at a local library, where he all but admitted that he was in, of and for the police department, made it clear that Fahey had truly hired a "company nigger." And in doing so, Fahey has alienated himself even further from the very community that put him into office.

And yet, he describes his decisions and appointments regarding both the Fire and Police Departments thusly:

> They are all committed to the concept of community
> policing and their support will allow us to move farther and
> faster than we have in the past. The Omaha Police and Fire
> Departments are some of the finest in the nation for two
> simple reasons – they are outstanding public servants
> dedicated to our community with strong committed
> leadership.

Farther and faster toward what end? He doesn't say because he doesn't know. But the police know: they view Fahey as a milquetoast who they can run over whenever they want to, and what they want to do is put as many black youth into jail as possible; every arrest means one more black kid with a police record. Every arrest has the potential to be upgraded to a Federal charge and, as a result, to overload the prison system so that the policymakers can influence the Legislatures to allocate more money for the construction of more detention centers, jails and prisons; all in small towns, all hiring nothing but white folks, folks who are too stupid to get jobs doing anything else, so they are hired to guard, harass and oversee black people.

And more white people are needed to make Omaha the kind of city whose population means that the city will get more Federal dollars. Here are Fahey's views on mergers and taxes:

> The climate has never been so ripe for merger in Omaha,
> Nebraska. Positive merger votes by the Douglas County
> Board and the Omaha City Council permit us for the first
> time our history, to begin the work to achieve mergers and
> efficiencies in the areas that make good sense. And that's
> great news for the taxpayers of Omaha and Douglas County.
> Making government more efficient and effective, and at the
> same time less expensive, must be our goal.

This is more evidence of the triage approach, an approach that has no room for the black community. This man talks about mergers, which means and includes annexing other communities. This increase the size of the city, but it also means extending services to those areas. This is why he is going to have a difficult time making government more efficient; the more they access, the more money it will cost them both in the short- and long-term. And when it comes to merging the County and the City services, there may be some scant savings somewhere down the road, but such a merger means re-tooling, re-defining and realigning both governmental entities. It also means layoffs and terminations, which is going to cost the city in terms of paying out unemployment compensation. These people are not thinkers, but they believe that if they use enough poly-syllabic words, the low-brown citizenry will just lose interest and turn away.

In a merger situation, as you annex new villages and areas, what happens is that there will invariably be less for each area and in a triage situation, the poorest areas receive little or nothing. So what is an "efficiency" for one entity (the City of Omaha) is a "nail in the coffin" for another area (North Omaha).

Fahey's thinking is not logical; it is short-term and it is dangerous. The following passage provides examples of this myopic vision:

> It's an opportunity we have to send a strong message to the
> entire state. We're pursuing the areas that make the most
> sense. What I call the "low hanging fruit" like the personnel,
> parks, planning and purchasing departments. The careful
> and thoughtful steps taken to merge these departments will
> lay the foundation for larger, more complicated mergers.

The low hanging fruit approach to anything is also known as a copout. An old statement teaches us that, "all rivers and most men, are crooked, because they choose the path of least resistance." That is what Fahey is all about and you just read his own words acknowledging the fact. "DO what is most expedient, what is the easiest." Forget about helping those who need the most help; help those who are already stable and in that way you can boast about having a great track record of success. Forget about doing the right thing, do the thing that is the most expedient.

While he is talking about merging departments in an attempt to look fiscally conservative and in charge, he is also placing people in charge of departments which shows how out of touch he is. One "negro" he appointed to head the Human Relations Department cut and ran, claiming he didn't feel well physically. But he feels good enough to run his own legal practice. The replacement is a woman who is even more shallow than the first appointment and take note that both appointments are people assigned to head the Human Relations Department. This is a department that should have the LARGEST budget in City Hall because there are so many acts of discrimination taking place around the city.

But they don't, and the reason is clear: the companies, businesses and corporations who are doing the discriminating are the same ones that endorse and donate money to the political campaigns of people like Fahey! That is why he puts DUNCES in charge of the Department, people who will not do what is right, but will – as he teaches – do what is politically expedient. The same strategy was taken by his Republican predecessor Hal Daub; that is why discrimination and racist activity is on the rise. Those who practice these evils know that when it comes to City Hall, they have the "go ahead"! The last several directors – from Kellie Paris Anaka and George Davis to Reginald Young and now Gail Thompson – have no love for the black community even though all of them are black. Their collective gutlessness and perfidy clearly pave the way for calls for a Latino/a or some other person of color to seize the reigns. These four people were and are, to put it mildly, miserable failures.

Fahey's poor decision making, rooted in laissez-faire management principles, outright cowardice and, of course, token patronage, can be seen in his following statement as well. He claims that,

> Not only is it important to streamline Omaha and Douglas County government services thereby creating amore responsive government, it's critical we begin thinking about how to grow and market this region. From our neighborhood communities to our business, development and tourism industry, our city county and region's future growth, development and vitality are dependent upon working together. Mergers are all about working together.

As if streamlining government is going to make it more responsive (while at the same time expanding the size of the city, enlarging it and exhausting city services), Fahey's mistakes continue. He wants to promote tourism (and even has an ad on television promoting Omaha and begging for convention business), but he wants to ignore a part of the city that is an available but unavailed of source of "cultural tourism:" the black community.

These backward Omahans want to promote a city atmosphere, but they want to remain small-time and small-town when it comes to their racist values. They want to talk about urban sophistication while displaying a Snuffy Smith-like backwardness in their relations with people who are ethically, racially and ideologically different from themselves. They want to talk about tourism when, only scant years ago, they had a law on the books forbidding back-to-back black concerts at the Civic Center. SO embarrassed were they about their racist policy that they had to undo it and then issue an apology to the superstar that they offended, none other than the great king of punk funk, Rich James!

Fahey continues by claiming,

> The Greater Omaha Convention and Visitors Bureau has assigned Omahans the task of selling their city to their professional organizations – and it's working. The GOCVB has booked 114 meetings and conventions – many of those sparked by local Hometown Heroes – citizens who have promoted their city. That generates more than 56,000 in hotel room nights and an economic impact of almost $41 million for our city. In 2004, Omaha, more and more, will be the place to be for conventions.

Fahey says that the Omaha Convention and Visitors Bureau has assigned the task of selling the city to their professional organizations. In other words, passing the buck – passing onto others that which is the OCVB's job! These professional organizations may be able to convince their national chapters to sponsor conventions here, but tourism is much more than that: it is creating harmony and security so that once people HEAR about Omaha, they will want to come, no matter WHAT organization they belong to!

This go out and "convince" people to come to Omaha is an activity that might serve for the time being; but if these hillbillies want a long-term commitment, they are going to have to change their 19th century attitudes on race, on social issues, on male-female relationships and the like, and become more open-minded to what is taking place in other parts of the world! Fahey's "patchwork approach" to tourism is *one more example of his short-sightedness and his tendency toward appeasing white groups instead of attacking essential social problems.*

Omaha will not be a place people want to come to when the world finds out how this city treats its black and Latino citizens. The word went national during the Al-Amin conflict; the word got out when Daub spent four years attempting to destroy North Omaha with his repressive police policies; the nation found out when the city's major newspaper sponsored a polygraph test, using an out of town firm, to confirm a racist white mayor who was running against a black woman. The nation is aware of the rise in guns and gangs in Omaha, Nebraska and in fact, Time magazine did a front-page story on it. And more recently, blacks around the country now know about the Omaha police and the abuse of search and seizure power during a DNA sweep that violated the rights of black men all over the city.

The local media does what it can to contain the racism of this city, knowing that if they record and report it, one of the larger affiliates might pick up a story and expose Omaha for what it is. That is why these stations keep their "community focus" programs confined to the personalities of people who don't know what the issues are: re-defining a once significant program on Channel 7 (KETV) so that now it is a roundtable that includes two white conservatives and a black host who can't control his show; bringing on an ignorant farm boy as Channel 3 (KMTV) has done with Travis Justice, and allow him to spew forth his specious and spurious "opinions" on a nightly basis; airing syrupy commitments to race relations as Channel 6 (WOWT) did several years back, knowing full well that station's racism led to the loss of the best black reporters in town (Ray Metoyer, Jon McCaa, etc.); and then Channel 42 (KPTM) that lacks any black anchors, no black reporters and an obvious affinity for the grandiose and inaccurate.

This is what Fahey's "patchwork tourism" has to deal with, and it one more reason why this city will always remain the punch line of one-liners and jokes on TV situation comedies. For instance, he grasps on to simplistic symbolism and attempts to pawn it off as substance in the following assertion:

> Have you noticed the red O!'s around town? It's all part of a community campaign led by the Greater Omaha Chamber of Commerce, Greater Omaha Convention and Visitors Bureau and the Mayor's office to generate excitement and pride. This couldn't be a better time as Omaha celebrates its 150th Birthday this summer.

This man thinks red "O!'s" are going to make Omaha more likeable to those that the city oppresses? The people at the Convention Bureau are making tens of thousands of dollars a year, and yet THIS is the best they can come up with? Here's what Fahey should do: disband the tourism department and merge it with the public relations office downtown. He should scrap those so-called "tourist experts' because they are not doing the job. He might want to consider creating a department of "Tourism and City Planning" and break up that "old boys network" that exists in the planning department, a group of people that have systematically raped North Omaha and done nothing more than mimick and copy that which they see taking place in other parts of the country. Until Fahey makes a definitive step and totally investigates his planning department and does something about the non-creative miscreants in the tourism division, the best he will be able to come up with regarding a descriptive slogan will be, "O-no!"

Omaha's celebration of its 150th birthday was as lily white as its day to day activities. Most of the people who live here are more than willing to adapt in exchange for the low cost of living and the laid-back atmosphere. But this is only another short-term solution: Omaha's political leadership is so backward that inevitably, more and more criminal activity will be uncovered at City Hall and beyond.

Fahey, obviously blind to these facts, continues his "State of the City" address with the following cheerleader-like statement:

> Omaha is on a roll and it's up to us to define our future.
> Some may see last year's riverfront redevelopment as a
> great conclusion. I see it as a launching pad for 2004 and
> beyond.

Fahey, attempting to sound upbeat, claims that the city is on a roll, but then says "it is up to us to define our future." And yet in all his speech, he has not given one inkling, one scintilla of a piece of evidence that the "we" is anybody more than white folks. He has offered no examples of cultural relativity, nothing inclusive and nothing remotely "human" when it comes to the attitudes that keep black people trapped socially, economically and politically. He totally mis-reads his own attempts at appointing credible people and has no idea of the negative impact that his appointments have had on the way that black people perceive City Hall. With such a track record, he is in no position to claim that he is defining anything more than white supremacy. If you can see the river, you can see North Omaha; but since the river can generate money and tourism for white folks, and all North Omaha does (thanks to a racist media) is scare those same white folks, use money to defend and develop the former, while denigrating and denying the latter. This is the only kind of "launching pad" Fahey could be talking about.

He then reiterates the mistakes made earlier:

> Above all else I will continue to fight tax increases by strictly
> controlling spending as we have for the past three years in a
> historically slow economy. I will concentrate my efforts on
> merging city and county government, from promoting
> neighborhood economic development plans to ensure their
> success, on strengthening our smaller business districts, and
> revitalizing our parks and public spaces.

Not one word about black folks. Not one word about dealing with the racist nature of society. Not one reference to a so-called, no longer heard about group called the Race Commission (remember THAT farce started by former mayor Daub?). There is nothing in his own words that would make black people feel as if they are a part of the city. He avoids referring to any of the many police-community related controversies that took place on his watch. And why should he? He avoided every single one of them.

He then winds down his speech talking about something he knows little about: urban planning. As he eloquently elucidates,

> The "cookie cutter" approach to planning won't work for Omaha as each community deserves and will get individual attention. I look forward to new design standards, so that while we not only grow our city, we also enjoy the urban environment too.

He lies. Each community didn't get individual attention – unless he considers neglect a form of attention. Because under his watch, that is what North Omaha received. He was visible for some fly by night, far too short community meetings, and his flunky Chris Rodgers, made some appearances with his usual, "I don't know, I'll ask the mayor and get back with you" responses. That is what Mike Fahey has contributed to North Omaha for the past four years. Following the lead of his corporate masters and business overseers he, like they, have only USED North Omaha when it came to securing Federal dollars that were then put to use in other parts of the City. The Planning Department's so-called "master plan" confirms what is alleged herein.

More of Fahey's address:

> I look forward to continued civility within City Hall and far beyond its walls. I look forward to Omaha making a tremendous mark on the national convention scene by attracting visitors from around the country.

Continued civility? That was a stab at Daub, and one of his campaign issues; Daub had divided the city and was a tyrant at City Hall. He was – and remains – a racist and this unified North Omaha as never before. Black people, for the most part, were able to repudiate and repel almost every racist trick Daub tried to implement. He was a racist and wasn't ashamed to show he was; his big mouth got him into trouble time and time again and enabled black people to come together in rage and revolt and deal with a man who obviously had major issues in the area of race.

So the vote of 2000 was not FOR Fahey – it as AGAINST Daub. And one of the points that Fahey kept mouthing was the issue of "restoring civility to city hall." But where Fahey fell short – and still falls short – is that he hasn't restored much of anything at City Hall. His so-called "Minority appointments," with the possible exception of Cecil Hicks, were a joke and indeed, were very similar to those made by his predecessor. Fahey just appointed more of them.

Secondly, Fahey hasn't done anything to bring "civility" to the white suburbs. They remain racist and ethnocentric. They remain hostile to low income housing. They still harbor a hatred for Senator Ernie Chambers who simply tells it like it is. Fahey cannot restore something in City Hall that does not exist in the context of where the people who work at City Hall reside. For him to believe that he could and then to claim that he could, once again shows an abysmal ignorance of a man who is more concerned with bricks, cement and construction than he is with human development.

His own speech makes it clear that the preceding allegation has merit. Fahey continues by uttering,

> I look forward to new and better recreational facilities, and working closely with the Greater Omaha Chamber and our business community to develop more retail opportunities, more jobs and affordable housing. I look forward to stronger, community focused public safety teams. And more work to strengthen after school programs. All of this, of course, with one goal in mind: making Omaha an even better place to live and work.

He says nothing about location when he's making promises along social lines, does he? New and better recreational facilities where? More retail opportunities, jobs and affordable housing – in what part of the city? He wants a strong, community focused public safety team – where will that be located? He wants after school programs – which schools? He wants to make Omaha a better place to live, but for whom? And if the answer is, "for everybody," then why doesn't he get more specific about the locations of these "visions" of his, since Omaha is racially and residentially segregated?

The speech mercifully concludes with Fahey telling the city that, "It's a pleasure to serve as your mayor. The future of our city is bright and the days ahead will be wonderful. Best wishes for a happy, healthy and prosperous new year. Thanks for your time this morning.

Geo-politics, buildings, arena convention centers, concerns about the airport and Abbott Drive, annexations, merging of city and county government. All of this and not one word about black folks. The only black person mentioned is an African-American police chief who is, by the chief's own words, is concerned more about law enforcement and understands his role than he is about black people. This same chief adds that he, "really doesn't compromise on that perspective."

Mayor Mike Fahey is a benevolent racist, not the aversive, dominative racist that his predecessor was. He let major issues fly by and didn't take a position. The black community is worse off now than it was four years ago when he became mayor. Downtown, west Omaha and the riverfront might be developed, but North Omaha remains nothing more than a scapegoat for more city-sponsored "programs" and buildings that only serve to remind North Omaha of its dependency and predicament.

In April of 2004, Fahey sent out invitations requesting, "the honor of your presence as the community celebrates the legacy of Dr. Martin Luther King, Jr. with the unveiling of "Rev. Dr. Martin Luther King, Jr.; I've Been to the Mountain Top" by sculptor Littlejohn Alston." The unveiling took place on April 24, 2004 at the Omaha/Douglas Civic Center (City Hall) and there was music and festivities. King's sellout son, Martin Luther King Jr. III was present at the time, and he gave a speech that was generic and boring, which of course, is what the white "doctor" ordered.

The statue was a joke. A local minister, Thomas Smith, was used as a model. The statue shows King running (from something) with a Bible in his hand. To add this insult to already obvious injury, on the invitations was a quote from Fahey:

> "Dr. Martin Luther King, Jr.'s life was about fighting for what this country was founded upon – fairness and equality for all. This statue will serve as a tribute to his work and a daily reminder for all of us to continue to fight for what is right."

Less than three months later, Fahey would be allowing Omaha police to stop and randomly administer DNA tests on any and all black men because of reports that a serial rapist had been victimizing women over the past several years. Fahey stepped in and did nothing while the cops, led by an Uncle Tom captain named Tommy Warren, denied black men of their rights until State Senator Ernie Chamber stepped in and rallied the community behind his efforts to call such unconstitutional police actions to a halt. Fahey's inaction was approval, a direct contradiction to the claims he made during the King unveiling.

These allegations, as can be seen, are based on Fahey's own words. They are the words of yet one more Mayor who made promises that he had no intention of keeping. ***And as a result, North Omaha has suffered for it.***

Know your opposition, and remember their words because they can come back to haunt you. But they can also be used against your opposition and that is what we are dealing with: oppositional relationships between the neighborhood and the city. It is a relationship that was created and has since been perpetuated by the city, the county and the state powers that be. They sat by idly and passed laws that maintained racial segregation for decades. Then, once we took the bull by the horns and turned that state of affairs around, they went to more subtle forms of showing how they hated black people: redlining, steering, housing discrimination, employment discrimination, financially opposing desegregation orders and so on.

Study the opposition and learn. Only then can you be successful and in doing so, create a context for "empowerment" of the community and in doing so, gain control over the context that controls the housing stock, the land and the people who live in and on both.

Three Approaches to Neighborhood Development

I have always informally credited black people with being the originators of the neighborhood movement. I say this because no matter what major city I visit or live in, there are neighborhood associations in black communities, some active and some not. But the key is that these are neighborhoods that were not always black; when our people entered, white folks left ("White flight") and this gave birth to the black ethnic enclaves that you see today.

It is my belief that the formalization of the neighborhood movement came about when outsiders saw the pride that we took in our homes and that indeed, certain sections of the black community were named and referred to by area, usually the street name or the name of some monument or building. Since we were compartmentalized anyway, those in power perhaps got the idea to start a movement (in much the same way they take the credit for inventing rock n' roll and jazz) that would create neighborhoods, with names. The final word is that in doing so, the area would be much easier to define and ultimately, control.

In this section there are three approaches other than the Africentric Sociourban Paradigm, are being defined: the social work approach, the neighborhood maintenance approach, and the political activist approach. We will begin with the neighborhood maintenance approach because long before there were these "gated communities" and "neighborhood watch" programs, black people were watching out for each other, having events and cleaning up the neighborhood.

The Neighborhood Maintenance Approach

The early editions of the *Omaha Star* newspaper carried a recurring college on the editorial page called "The Roving Reporter." This was no fluff piece; the questions that were asked were hard core questions and are surely even need of answering even today, more than 70 years later.

In the August 20, 1938 issue, the question posed was, "Do you think North Twenty-fourth street is properly lighted as compared to other neighborhood business sections of the city? To this day, no newspaper poses questions to its readership because, for the most part, they don't care what their readers think – or want. At that time (unlike now) those in charge of the Omaha Star were engaged in community involvement and as a result, they were – in the tradition of the black press – advocates and defenders of black people.

This question posed goes directly to the issue of "place framing," which is what Deborah Martin (2003) outlines in an article titled, "Place-Making: Constituting a Neighborhood for Organizing and Activism." A point where I agree with Martin is where she outlines how space – that is, the setting, geographic location, and socio-spatial context of a neighborhood – influences the formation of collective identities and activist agendas (p. 731). And that is what North Omaha has done for the past decade: provided a "culture" for black people to insulate themselves from the racism that permeates the rest of Omaha. No matter how well off you are of who you think you are – or who you marry – if you're black, you'll come back to North Omaha because, thanks to racial and residential segregation, that is where the "flavor" and the "soul" are at.

This is how the North Omaha community – the ghetto – gave form and function to a number of organizations and efforts that met the needs of the people of various time periods. In this case, the answers to the questions posed by the "Roving Reporter" provide an idea as to what was going on in the minds of ghetto residents and shows that we did not childishly sit around waiting for the white man to come around and give us ideas.

For instance James "Jimmy" Jewell, then the owner of Tuxedo Billiard Parlor, answered, "I think we are slighted as far as lighting facilities are concerned, North 24th Street from Cuming to Lake is not only poorly lighted (sic), but is the last area to be lighted (sic) and the first to have the lights turned off."

Now why would this be the case? Because when services are deteriorating, black people find out first because they deteriorate in our area first. When services are lacking, they begin lacking first in the black community. When Cox Cable came to town, the last area (hub) to get the optimum channels was North Omaha. When Northwestern Bell came, it was North Omaha that was last to get call waiting, call forwarding and the other amenities that those living out west got from the get-go.

Mr. R. Taylor of the Lux Barber Shop said, "I feel we need quite a bit of improvement. It would add a great deal to our business as well as to the appearance of North Twenty-Fourth Street." Mr. J.H. Anderson of Climax Cleaners replied, "That is the first thing I noticed when I came to Omaha – the poor lighting system on North Twenty-fourth street, and I think something ought to be done to improve this condition." Those from outside of Omaha can get a quick understanding of the disdain that the rest of the city has for the part of the area where black people live.

It becomes clear right away. But white people don't see it because, in their view, black people get what they deserve. The problem with that statement is that far too many white people in Omaha – perhaps the majority – get far more than they deserve.

People don't have to be literate or eloquent to be able to describe their surroundings and the feelings or "vibes" that they get from those surroundings.

Today, as white folks in neighborhood associations apply for and receive grant money for neighborhood watches, garbage cleanup and other minor details, inner city neighborhood groups like the Ideal Improvement Club in the 1920s and today's own Highlander, Wirt-Binney-Spencer, and Triple One neighborhood groups deal with inner city issues, which include violence and crime. And again, our ideas as far back as 1928 generated questions and answers that are now being put into effect by those who live OUTSIDE of the area.

Want proof? The August 27, 1928 edition of the *Omaha Star's* "Roving Reporter" question was, "What is the best means of eliminating the congregation of boys around our business establishments?" Here are some of the answers.

Mr. A.B. Wright of 2872 Maple said, "What we need to eliminate this congregating is adequate amusements for our young people, like the whites – in the form of swimming pools, playgrounds, tennis courts, and a first class YMCA and YWCA. We are taxed the same sin most instances more than the white people and should have the same consideration for our young people in return for our taxes." Miss Annie Franklin of 3026 "R" Street said, "In order to keep the boys from hanging around business establishments I would suggest more activities at the Recreational centers and nearby parks should be erected."
Mr. C.B. Mayo of 2422 Lake Street replied, "I don't think resorting to law enforcement would e right, because these boys have to have some place to meet, but there should be some adequate form of clean amusements, like playgrounds, and a YMCA to occupy their time."

These ideas are the seeds of what you see today. While neglected by white planners, black people knew had to be done, knew what their rights were and knew that "an idle mind is the devil's workshop." And at least one respondent knew the importance of listening to the young people: "The best way is to have a large social to get them together and reason with them. Let them express their opinion and offer suggestions to find some other means of amusements. And if that would to help, then we should resort to the force of the law." Mr. Charles Walls, a butcher, said, "First you should explain to the boys what harm they are doing to the business by hanging around; and if they fail to heed to your advice, use other devices."

Take notice that the tendency is to look inward first, then rely on outside forces if need be – it appears to be the other way around here in the 21st Century, where black people appear all too eager to bring in racist cops to deal with nuisance issues.

What was just described was the grass roots version of the "neighborhood maintenance approach." Neighborhood specialists Fraser & Kick (2005) define it somewhat differently:

> **The neighborhood maintenance approach** has focused on protecting neighborhoods from perceived and actual threats … Some strategies community groups have employed include peer pressure, political lobbying and legal-juridicial (sic) action. The organizing of community for neighborhood-level improvement and maintenance has been a strategy to assist middle and upper classes as well as in lower-income areas (emphasis original)

When it comes to the low-income neighborhood associations, much of what is described above does not really apply. The "perceived threats" are real when it comes to black people: we don't hallucinate nor are we paranoid schizophrenics. We have endured over 350 years of white abuse, much of it taking place in segregated and/or separated racial enclaves similar to those now being euphemistically described as "neighborhoods." We don't cry "wolf" because, in most cases, the person answering the call – a cop, for instance – is also a part of the reason we are shouting for help in the first place.

Secondly, the idea of "political lobbying" is not an approach that we use in the formal sense of the term. Our version of lobbying, which has bought great success in terms of accomplishing our goals, I might say, revolves around "boycotts," "pickets," "protests" and the like. This is the ultimate lobbying that goes beyond the backroom deals that white suburbanites, because of their contacts and because politicos tend to live in those kinds of communities, practice and promote.

Also in regard to neighborhood maintenance, the authors opine,

> Regardless of the type of neighborhood, organizing community toward enhancing, maintaining and protecting neighborhood space has been tied closely to land-use decision making and enforcement … An estimated one-third of new housing units built in the U.S. since 1970 have included some form of privatized community association. In lower income neighborhoods community based organizations have organized against unwanted land use as well (Fraser & Kick, p. 26)

I'm not sure if the preceding statement is quite accurate. The authors claim that, "Regardless of the type of neighborhood, organizing community toward enhancing, maintaining and protecting neighborhood space has been tied closely to land-use decision making and enforcement." The type of neighborhood determines how much attention it will get from the city. That, in turn, is based on how much priority the city attributes to that neighborhood. Need may not have anything to do with it: most black communities are in need, but they get ignored anyway as outside developers buy up land and then sit on it. And, of course, cities ignore certain areas so that they will remain unkempt, undesirable and crime-ridden, which, in turn, generates even more Community Development Block Grants and Community Service Block Grants.

Moreover, the previous statements says that organizing community toward enhancing, maintaining and protecting neighborhood space has been "tied closely" to land-use decision making and enforcement. Again, I beg to differ. What these scholars want us to believe is that what they write are uniform facts and are therefore universally applicable; such is not the case. Those communities with wherewithal and a chance for immediate growth receive the most attention. This is called "the triage approach," akin to a triage unit in the military that helps those patients that have the best chance of surviving. The rest are placed on the back burner, that is, if they are ever helped at all.

Taking over the neighborhood movement is where the real funding is going. One way is by "consolidating" them all, or, as the previous excerpt bore out, simply creating "some form of privatized community association." This is an overseer that will dictate what you can and cannot do to your property and so on. This is not the type of "neighborhood maintenance" program that black people need. This is more of a "fortress" type situation, managed communities high on security and usually gated. One article I read long ago referred to them as "community of interest," where people of similar demographics (elderly, women, single parents, etc.) live in a secured and enclosed area where supermarkets, movie theatres and schools are all provided.

That is what "neighborhood maintenance" has come to: low on the "neighborhood" concept (after all, segregation is segregation) and high on the "maintenance," which means control, surveillance and monitoring. Big Brother has arrived.

The Social Work Approach

In the field of social work there is an approach known as the "strengths/empowerment approach. I would like to briefly share this because it appears to be more in line with what the black community should do and has the potential to do than these "wait for us to build another park" approach that is now being employed in and around North Omaha.

> At the heart of the strengths perspective is a belief in the basic goodness of humankind, a faith that individuals, however downtrodden or debilitated, can discover strengths in themselves that they never knew existed … No matter how little or how much may be expressed at one time … people often have a potential that is not commonly realized. A belief in human potential is tied to the notion that people have untapped, undetermined reservoirs of mental, physical, emotional, social and spiritual abilities which can be mobilized in times of need .. tapping into not what is but what can be. (Van Wormer & Boes, 1998—emphasis original).

This is what I was talking about when I held three "self-empowerment" conferences at the turn of the century. I believe that black people are the strongest people on this earth, and I believe that of that group, African-Americans are even stronger because of that 400 year slavery episode. We may have survived it physically, but we remain scarred because we were never "de-briefed" afterwards. That is a story for another time.

At this juncture we continue to doubt our own power where it matters most. Far too many of us continue to believe that, "The white man's ice is colder than our ice." As the excerpt states, "people often have a potential that is not commonly realized." In our case, that potential has been suppressed by a society that only wants to funnel and focus our powers on bullshit activity: sports, singing, dancing and other forms of entertainment. I believe that we have latent and untapped talent that can enable us to re-create North Omaha in our own image and interests. If others want to help with technical assistance, financing and perhaps some consultation, that is fine: but they have to also be willing to practice non-intervention and watch while we solve our own problems.

To date, they have not been willing to do so. Instead, we are force-fed "hope" and "wishes" and "prayers:"

> Every community, every narrative needs a note of hope. In our own fields and our own ways, we must convey hope … Believing that it can be done, that we can move forward, that people will care, and that we will turn things around is contagious. (Hardcastle, et. al., 2004: p. 217).

There is a time and a place for prayer, hope and wishing. When that time is ill-conceived, and when we opt to engage in these actions instead of watching our backs while other people talk about "empowering" us, we are making a grave mistake, one that we have, unfortunately, made for hundreds of years when it comes to Caucasian people. We trust them and they know that; and that is why the social work approach works so well on us: they have a god complex and a missionary syndrome; to many of us suffer from what psychologist Roderick W. Pugh called, "The-we-ain't-ready-syndrome," along with low self-esteem and serious cases of learned helplessness. Combine these two different areas of thought from these two different groups and what do you have? Slavery, 2012. How then, can we believe that these "empowerment movements" are for our (black) benefit?

We are treated like children who need to be helped, like problems that have yet to be solved. As Gary and Littlefield posit,

> Although Billingsley (1968, 1988) and Hill (172) have documented the strengths of African-American families, the prevailing paradigm for assessment and intervention with *this group is problem focused and deficit oriented. African-American families are generally treated as flawed and dysfunctional units;* little regard is paid to their strengths. Moreover, traditional treatment models are limited in that intervention is *problem specific* (Gary & Littlefield, 1998: 81- emphasis added).

The same applies in the areas of neighborhood development. We are viewed as people to be "taught," "helped," "shown the way." Even the token developers that the city fronts money to and uses to make it appear as if they know what they're doing get no real respect: jive-time, small-time, color-filled projects that are usually nothing more than fodder for the white man's barroom jokes and after-dinner meetings with his cronies.

The social work approach has its positives, but not when the race relations of the players are so skewed and one-sided. Here is how the social work approach is defined by Fraser & Kick:

> The social work approach has focused on service delivery through neighborhood-based organizations … Significant resources were provide to low-income families, including day-to-day maintenance services, human capital development opportunities (e.g., education) and opportunities for activity in political and intellectual movements centered on issues of race, class and gender … Led by the Progressives such as Robert Wood and Jane Addams, the social work approach

identified the neighborhood as an appropriate level at which to
organize and test social reforms, but in many ways it left the
politics of reconciliation between labor and capital to others
(Fraser & Kick, pp. 25-26)

Again, their overview is not totally accurate or attributable to the neighborhood context when the variable of "race" is added.

From the top down, those doing the "servicing" and the "delivering" are not African-Americans. They may be ordering around a few people who are black – the way the Nebraska Department of Social Services did when it was closing down black day care centers a few years back – but other than that, the key is to associate all that is about "social" and "welfare" with that which is white. In that way, black youth can grow up seeing white people, not their parents, as their guardians and saviors. Again, Caucasians think in long-range terms (e.g., marathons); black folks, because of our precarious position and condition, have to be concerned about the short-term (sprints) and as such, continue to be open for tricks and scams perpetrated by "service deliverers."

The social work approach is paternalistic and insultingly dominating. Things may have calmed down in the last few years, but ask the sisters who were on welfare what those white social workers put them through. The system itself is rife with rules that are nearly impossible to follow, and even now, with public housing, there is "zero tolerance." What happens when those individuals, like most human beings, make a simple mistake? They're out on the street, that's what.

The social work approach appears to be the approach being used by Nebraska's economic developers in general and the city of Omaha's planning department, in particular – especially as it relates to community and neighborhood development planning. And here's the part where a lack of cultural competency is most clear on the part of the writers. They claim that, *the social work approach identified the neighborhood as an appropriate level at which to organize and test social reforms, but in many ways it left the politics of reconciliation between labor and capital to others.*

What was the process used by social workers to "identify" the neighborhood as the "test entity"? What logic would that make, since the neighborhood is a microcosm of the immediate community in which it is located? For instance, one might take the Triple One neighborhood and work within its boundaries, but there is still an entire North Omaha community that suffers just as much as those in the "68111" zip code! What about 68110? What about 68104 and 68131?

The neighborhood was nothing more than an easy to control area that could be used as a "laboratory" for social workers and their minions to conduct various "social experiments" on what far too many people in the social science field believe to be nothing more than "human black lab rats." This nation's history provides ample evidence that such a perception has always existed and in the scientific community persists to this day.

And where are these "politics of reconciliation"? Are we to believe that because two groups "collaborate" that there has been some type of reconciliation between the two. Maybe the black side of the equation, in Omaha, has led the whites with the power (on the other side) to believe as much. But the fact is, reconciliation is defined as, "restoring of harmony, adjustment of differences." In Omaha, you cannot restore that which never existed in the first place. The history of whites and blacks, North Omahans and the rest of the city, has been, at best, antagonistic. As for an "adjustment of differences," why would whites with power decide to "change" when their attitudes and actions toward black people, including segregation, discrimination and racist application of the law, have generated billions of dollars and one of the highest standards of living in the United States?

So there is no reconciliation between labor and capital when it comes to "others." The "others" – the ones who remain under-capitalized and unemployed – are fodder on which labor and capital feed!

What is more accurate, in my view, is the social work paradigm that continues to view the black community, black families, black men, women and children, as some type of "problem." They have coined such terms as "tangle of pathology," and "culture of poverty." Put another way,

> Deficit, disease, and dysfunction metaphors permeate treatment at every stage of the process, from intake to termination (Cowger, 1994). In the criminal justice system, clients often find their very selfhood defined by their crimes. For such persons, whose views of therapy and of all authority figures are apt to be decidedly negative, a positive approach is essential to establish the one crucial ingredient of effective treatment -- trust. Sometimes one encounter or one supportive relationship -- whether with a teacher, social worker, or priest -- can offer a turning point in a life of crime (Van Wormer & Boes, 1998).

For over a century, with the on-going racist laser-focus of the major newspaper, Omaha's black community has been stigmatized as a crime-ridden war zone with no prospects. The city administration has only acted with sincere benevolence when there was a riot or a threat of one. To this day, it is clear that North Omaha remains stigmatized, which is why these people who are accepting "collaborative efforts" from so-called black leaders do so only when they can pick and choose the "negroes' they want to have interactions with. In Omaha, most white people fear North Omaha, and that is why the deficit model described above in regard to criminals and inmates, can be applied to all of North Omaha because, in the views of the majority population, that's what we are.

This view of North Omaha as a crime zone and blacks as criminals aids and abets in the "angelic" and "missionary" vision of the social worker and the social work approach. These are people who believe that blacks have to be "saved" and "salvaged."

The social work approach is one that is more about paternalism and control than it is about helping the neighborhoods and communities that need help the most.

The Political Activist Approach

I consider myself an activist but I wouldn't use it as a descriptor because, like words like "militant" and "nationalist," you do more to scare your own people than you do white folks. Black people, so brainwashed for so long, have equated having a black viewpoint with being anti-white. Why, I ask, must whites always be a part of your intellectual or perceptual equation? Can't you just love your own people so much that you just don't have time or room for them? That is the kind of "politics" that I'm talking about: helping those that need help the most and, as you know, that means us.

According to the definition by Fraser & Kick, however, the political activist approach,

> … has focused on changing the institutional structures that are viewed as causing poverty and the declining conditions of neighborhoods … Not infrequently they have challenged the existing power structure by developing a community based upon socioeconomic "class consciousness" or based on other identities that have not been expressed spatially in terms of a geographical neighborhood (Fraser & Kick, pp. 26-27).

As usual, these men avoid the issues of race. You cannot talk about "class" without talking about race in America. Many of the poor are black and most of the black are poor – it doesn't get any simpler than that. Furthermore, and as I've always said and believed, there are poor white people – but they ain't poor because they're white!

Changing the institutional structures has not been a priority for several reasons. For one, institutions are designed to perpetuate, not condemn, themselves. So if you want to change an institutional arrangement, the best thing to do is to create what I call "counter-institutions" and deal from a position of power. Individuals, no matter how strong, cannot overcome institutions. You can cite the case of the civil rights movement, but that movement did not change institutions: it simply said, "scoot over – I want to share it with you." That is not even close to the revolutionary bent of groups like the Revolutionary Action Movement, the Weathermen, the Brown Beret or, to a lesser extent, the grandiose Black Panther Party for Self-Defense.

I also differ when they write that political activists have challenged the existing power structure "by developing a community based upon socioeconomic "class consciousness" or based on other identities that have not been expressed spatially in terms of a geographical neighborhood." These identities have been expressed spatially and for that matter, temporally (based on time) as well. Race and class are definers and have an impact on the geographic area. That is what segregation is all about: those in power take race and class and use it to determine what geographic area you are going to occupy: near the bottoms (where the floods take place), close to railroad tracks and noise, near toxic waste dumps and so on. These are but a few examples of "identities that are expressed spatially even though the defining of that space is in the hands of the powers that be (e.g., planners, developers, real estate experts, etc.)

Deborah Martin (2003) outlined a concept called "place-framing." She believes that the neighborhood functions as a site of political activism and further that, "Neighborhood-level activism in the U.S. urban areas increasingly operates in a political context dominated by an elite agenda of urban growth through civic boosterism and redevelopment projects (p. 731).

This is one way to put it; a more accurate way would to say that neighborhood-level activist in the United States inner cities (black and Latino communities) increasingly operates in a political context *dominated by neglect by the elite decision makers whose agenda it is to keep the areas poor* until such time as they can attract enough poverty grant money to relocate those populations and prepare those neighborhoods for the return of their elite counterparts (e.g., white folks).

That "civil boosterism" and those "redevelopment projects" that were referred to are just part of the smokescreen that those in power use to rationalize their incursions into low-income areas. That "boosterism" is nothing but a public relations campaign by the local media to provide support for the "new programs that are on the way," and the "redevelopment projects" are just that: projects aimed at "developing all over again," meaning a re-definition of the area in the image and interests of those who are in power. The indigenous populations, by way of other prongs of the "redevelopment plan," are therefore relocated to other parts of the city through eminent domain, scattered-site housing, apartments that offer affordable housing and other "redevelopment plans" aimed at inducing the poor to move to places that are more "in line with their incomes" and therefore leave the central city to those who want to develop it because of access to a riverfront, a lakefront, downtown jobs, downtown night leisure and other reasons.

A book titled, **Asset Building and Community Development** offers us an explanation as to why people get involved in neighborhood groups:

> Research shows that length of residence and interests in protecting the value of the home are strong predictors of membership in neighborhood associations. Having children younger than age 5 also strongly affects membership in these organizations; presumably, interests in safety and education are the motivating factors in this case (Green & Haines, 2002: 72).

The preceding definition falls short. While having children who are young and concerns about the community are important, what about the political issues? *People who join neighborhood associations are people who want to get involved in addressing problems – and prospects – taking place in the community.* Those problems are, at their foundation, usually political in nature.

Then there is the statement by Martin that "place informs social action." While I agree that this might be the case in most instances, it is social action of some kinds that define place. For instance, there would be no "black community" in Omaha were it not for white flight. Therefore the actions of those who wanted to leave the area gave birth to a community that is now known across the state as the "near Northside" of Omaha. So action precedes place, and once place is established, more action is needed and used to either maintain a place or relocate it.

This is where political activism begins and ends: addressing the time, place and circumstance under which behaviors take place, behaviors that may shape policies and laws that are imposed on neighborhoods. Any political activist has the right to analyze, then address, what those policies and laws are.

Finally, in regard to the political activist approach, Fraser & Kick opine,

> The political activist approach to organizing neighborhood community has arguable declined in prevalence since the 1970s, as global recession motivated U.S. corporations to move offshore, and the state began to dismantle social welfare programs (i.e., emergent neoliberalism). In accord with the neo-liberalist response to urban problems in the late 1970s and 1980s, the state has significantly decreases funding for programmatic efforts aimed at inner city neighborhoods specifically, and urban areas more generally … Together, these

factors have shaped current configurations of neighborhood-
based organizing, spurring community building as the dominant
strand of supported neighborhood organizing (pp. 28-29)

The political activist approach to organizing neighborhood and community has not declined or increased except in response to the conditions of that particular neighborhood or community.

For instance, in the previous excerpt, the author claims that political activism has declined. What is this premise based on? Did they conduct a survey or study? Who did these men talk to? If they are so certain, then why would they then add the qualifier, "arguably" in regard to the alleged decline? And why would political activism decline since the 1970s when, since that time, conditions that negatively impact upon neighborhoods and communities have grown worse, especially since the two terms of Ronald Reagan, the two terms of George Bush, and two terms of George W. Bush? Even under Clinton, political activism, especially as it had to relate to the police and to Clinton's personal issues, was flourishing.

What reasons do Fraser and Kick give for this alleged decline in political activism? Their reasoning is based on their claims that it was because of a global recession, dismantling of welfare and corporations moving offshore. Don't they know that "all politics is local"? Don't they know that the issues they've raised are moot when it comes to the low income because, for the most part, low-income minorities are always living in a "depression" or a "recession." The end to welfare did not hurt, because the money is still coming (if you can find a job), and so is the Section 8 housing subsidy and the food stamps. Poor people are not panicking because they've always been poor; political activism is not waning because the people they advocate for, those same low-income people, remain poor and in need of a voice!

Community-building, as they call it, is a term that places the macro- above the individual needs of residents. How can you build a community without first of all focusing on the individuals, families and neighborhoods that make up that community? Community-building sounds good, but it exists only on the aerial maps and drafting tables of urban planners. They can talk about it in such generic terms because the impact of what is taking place in those neighborhoods and communities *does not directly affect them!*

Since I have refuted the "factors" that the authors claim "shaped current configurations of neighborhood based organizing," then their claim of community building being "spurred" as the dominant type of neighborhood organizing is also incorrect. It may be the preferred type as outlined by the city officials, urban planners, and others, but in the world of application and practicality, political activists are still about organizing small pockets of groups with similar interests and putting pressure on the status quo. It is about confidence-building, coalition-building, and consciousness-raising; if these are successful, *then you have the basis for a grass roots movement* – real community-building.

AFRICENTRIC SOCIOURBAN PLANNING = "RE-EDUCATION

One of the reasons for the success of the Triple One Neighborhood Association was the subsequent creation of the Triple One Parents' Union, which immediately went to the rescue of black students who were, on varying levels, being abused by the Omaha Public Schools.

As I wrote earlier in this book, In sum, the Africentric Sociourban Paradigm is an idea whose time has come and rests on a present-day as well as a futuristic tenet – leadership by people of color FOR people of color with the future of a "browning of America" being inevitable. White people can no longer teach what they don't know and lead what they don't know, as has been the traditional tendency and historical pattern.

The youth are our future and if we defend and develop them, we automatically pave the way for on-going progress. But it has to be done on a playing field that we control and/or have major input into. We have to be able to reject, in detail, defiance and self-determination, the vile and vulgar images and assertions imposed on us by the educational system. They can only teach what they know: and when it comes to cultural inclusion or relativity, they know very little.

Our young people – the students in this educational system - are also victims of stereotype-related maltreatment. **Racism then, perpetuates stigma.** A book titled *Crisis in Black and White* bought out some interesting points in 1964. The author, Charles Silberman, wrote,

> ... For one thing, the children become aware almost from
> infancy of the opprobrium Americans attach to color. They
> feel it in their parents' voices as they are warned to behave
> when they stray beyond the ghetto's wall. They become
> aware of it as they begin to watch television, or go to movies,
> or read the mass-circulation magazines; beauty, success, and
> status all wear a white skin. (Silberman, 1964: p. 48)

Although simplistic, it makes the point. These are issues that far too many of us do not discuss with our kids. When Triple One was going to meetings with teachers and school board members, the parents would be sitting right there, afraid to say much of anything. We had to be their voice because what the children were experiencing is the same thing, to a greater extent, that their parents had also faced when they went to school. And what was that, you ask?

> They learn to feel ashamed of their color as they learn to talk
> and thereby to absorb the invidiousness our very language
> attaches to color. White represents purity and goodness,
> black represents evil. The white lie is the permissible
> misstatement, the black lie the inexcusable falsehood; the
> black sheep is the one who goes astray (and when he goes
> astray, he receives a black mark on his record); defeat is
> black (the stock market crashed on "Black Thursday"),
> victory white ... (Silberman, 1964: pp. 49-50)

Therefore, to have power, we have to first of all gain power over our own minds and what we "feed" those minds. It is not enough to be in the community organizing while our children enter schools that feed them pablum about how great white people are. This would create conflict within our families and self-esteem issues in the hearts and actions of our future generations. That is why community work, a form of education in itself, has to nevertheless be connected with a "re-education" campaign because the battle for the minds of the people is, as Mao taught, the first half of the struggle.

At the core of community and neighborhood development issues are issues of differing perspectives on what is "good" for our communities. These differing definitions are based on race, and the racial differences are rooted in different types of symbolism. Again, Silberman:

> The symbolism which elevates white and debases black
> inevitably affects the consciousness of every person, white
> or black ... This arrangement of things [is] communicated
> to all in our culture by all its modes and means, passed by
> osmosis through all the membrances of class, caste and
> color of relationships, caressingly and painlessly injected
> into our children by their school texts and, even more, their
> story books ... (Silberman, 1964: p. 114)

Having been a graduate student in one of the top urban education programs in the nation at the University of Wisconsin-Milwaukee, I learned and studied a great deal about how to change the structure of American education. What they taught me is what I turned around and improved. It was what I learned creating the Triple One Parents Union and organizing in the Omaha community that I wrote about and used in my classroom debates, not the other way around.

At any rate, a key aspect of "re-education" is not only aimed at young people, but also at the teachers themselves – they must be "de-racicized:"

> ... teacher education that embraces an anti-racist perspective
> recognizes that prospective teachers' and teachers'
> sensibilities are shaped by the same forces that mold us in the
> society at large ... However' antiracist educators understand
> racism as learned behavior and, as such, it can be unlearned
> (Ladson-Billings, 2000: 211).

These movements – working in the schools to change the teacher attitudes and the curriculum – can run concurrently with the work being done in the community, just as I did with the Triple One Neighborhood Association and then the Triple One Parents Union, later combining the names (and functions) to become TONAPU -- the Triple One Neighborhood Association and Parents Union.

ESSAYS AND EXPOSURE: TWO ARTICLES FROM 1982

Two examples from leadership in the know embody what my proposed Africentric Sociourban Paradigm is all about. Both were written thirty-six (36) years ago, one by an African-American state senator from Nebraska and the other from this writer.

Chambers Responds to NOCD's Tyler

This was a point well-established by a rebuttal written by Senator Ernie Chambers, that appeared in the January 20, 1982 edition of the major newspaper. The text of Chambers' essay well documents the role that the city and NOCD played in bilking the government, misinforming the black community, and generally playing games with community projects such as a "black fence" that encircled the old Safeway Building. The fence was removed once Chambers pointed out how foolish and racist the move was.

Now, the essay:

> In "Another Point of View" (Dec. 21) Carl Tyler, president
> of North Omaha Community Development (NOCD) purported to
> respond to my remarks about NOCD's involvement in the "fence
> and park hoax" at 24th and Lake. My reply to him is delayed
> because information I requested Dec. 22 from Omaha Housing and
> Community Development Director Marty Shukert reached my
> office Jan. 7. Summarized at the end of this article, it gives food

for thought as to why NOCD often assumes the role of apologist for the city.

Mr. Tyler expressed a "wish to set the record straight" because "Senator Chambers made a number of untrue statements." Rather than lay a single untrue statement at my door, he accused The World-Herald of misrepresenting NOCD and executive director George Garnett through "misquotes," "misinterpretations" and "false illustrations."

It is puzzling why NOCD made no whisper of challenge nor sought to "set the record straight" on any of The World Herald's alleged iniquities at the time of **commission;** and when NOCD did decide to object, it was under the guise of accusing me of untrue statements!

*   *   *

The allegedly false illustration accompanied an article extolling redevelopment of 24th and Lake, and NOCD's involvement. NOCD sought no correction, though it's likely that it clipped the article.

While declaring that a park the size depicted in The World-Herald drawing would "eliminate a major (?) manufacturing plant and the jobs that go with it," Mr. Tyler did not "set the record straight" on whether the jobs held are held by community residents **nor** that Canar may soon vacate, despite the enhancement of his property with public funds. Though disclaiming involvement in a "court settlement" that allowed a new face to be erected, Mr. Tyler did not "set the record straight" with an explanation of why NOCD concealed information it possessed about the new fence, and accepted misguided media and public praise for "bringing down" the old one.

Nor was the record "set straight" by disclosing that the Garden Apartments' remodeled units have been priced out of the range of those people whose depressed economic condition provided the **qualifying basis** for the federal UDAG grant which fueled the scheme.

*   *   *

Regarding the North Freeway, Mr. Tyler did not "set the record straight" by disclosing that I provided NOCD and the public with more crucial information than any other source and forced many concessions. His suggestion that I "help plan" any project that is destructive of the black community is traitorous and irrational. I was invited "to become a part of the problem-solving process." The invitation revealed two things:

(1) Abysmal ignorance of the profound political **and** problem-solving significance of my legislative success in obtaining district election of the school board and the City Council; and,

(2) An inexplicable forgetfulness of my intervention in **their** behalf to help solve problems NOCD was having with the City Council and Gov. Thone's office (from which they had been effectively barred).

From Marty Shukert came information establishing a heavy financial tie justifying the characterization of NOCD as an **adjunct** to the city. Since 1977, the city has funneled loans and grants to NCOD totaling $2,046,936. Of that amount, $32,127 was a **grant** to rehabilitate the NOCD building owned by NOCD president Carl Tyler. Another $114,000 in grants went primarily for NOCD salaries. As a **moneyless** "co-developer" of the Garden Apartments, and a shill for Greater Omaha Corporation, NOD received a **grant** of $850,000 and a loan of $300,000 at 3 percent, and a share of the **title.**

As the **moneyless** sole developer of the Blue Lion Project at 24th and Lake, the NOCD will receive a grant of $400,000 and a **loan** of $300,000 and the **title.**

The total amount is public funds. With income derived from the projects, NOCD is empowered by the city to select which persons and projects will receive funds for 'redevelopment" purposes.

Under such a sweet relationship, it is impossible to ignore the truisms that "the hand that feeds, controls" and "the servant does not bite the hand that feeds."

Now the record has been set straight.

Minorities Could Help Build Omaha

In June of 1982, my first teaching stint was over, but I still had a lot to say and to contribute. The World-Herald printed an essay that I sent them, and, for once, spelled all the words the way I wrote them, didn't edit our key sections and gave it a fairly positive headline. When " 'Minorities Could Help Build Omaha'" appeared on page 7 in the June 7, 1982 issue, I was pleasantly surprised:

The writer is an instructor in the Black Studies Department at the University of Nebraska at Omaha
By Matthew C. Stelly

During these tumultuous times, the latent and untapped talent in the Omaha community should have priority over all other arenas. If the "survival" of the city is our primary concern, the following concepts and characteristics should be taken into maximal consideration.

If we add up the monies spent on "outside consultants" since the year 1979, we can already see capital flowing outside of our city. For example, Adam Pinsker

– a "consultant" from New York – has already received over $35,000 from our city's Chamber of Commerce, local businessmen, Creighton University and the Metropolitan Arts Council. In its quest for a "United Arts Fund," the chamber committee spent an additional $41,500 for a C.W. Shavers report.

The Department of Housing and Community Development gave the Real Estate Research Corporation of Chicago $8,500 in 1980 to do a study on the Garden Apartments. In 1981 this same research group was given another $25,765 to do a market analysis of 24th and Lake Streets. Between 1979 and 1981, the "North Omaha Plan" has cost over $90,000. Again, outsiders – these from Berkeley, Calif. – took the money and ran.

These approximated figures (approximated because they are underestimated) total $200,765 spent since 1979 alone. While these economic realities might sound worthwhile to many Omahans, there are certain ideological considerations that are implied by such actions.

First of all, money is flowing out of the city at a time when Mayor Boyle claimed he would seek to bring business in. How can he – or anyone – do that when the basis of any successful business venture is, indeed, an environment where there is economic stability? And how can we become economically stable when we do not use our own internal resources during fact-finding or other types of endeavors?

Secondly, while the city and others seem content with spending money on outside consultants and analysts, Omahans face an economic crunch which manifests itself in a myriad of ways.

There is rising unemployment in the city, particularly among minority youth; cutbacks in student loans and grants have forced area corporations and charitable trusts to design and develop scholarship programs; retrenchment tactics by area corporations and educational institutions further exacerbate the employment arena and new starts for housing are at a standstill citywide.

These realities call for a "survival program" that is comparatively inexpensive and which makes use of an available – but unavailed of – source of talent, creativity and energy: the "minority communities" of Omaha.

Quiet as it is kept, it was a minority organization that gave rise to the new Minority Policy Panel of the Nebraska Arts Council; quiet as it is kept, it was a black man – Sen. Ernie Chambers – who made the Economic Task Force as functional as it was; quiet as it is kept, it was a black campus group – B.L.A.C. – that was the foundation and background for today's Student Programming Organization.

These are only a few of the many examples of how minority persons – adept at surviving because of the conditions we live under – can "consult" the majority population in this city on how it, too, can learn to survive.

Through this process of practice, we will 1) promote a collective vocation between the majority and minority communities in this city; 2) we will save the city money because no longer will we have a call on outsiders to come and find solutions for us; 3) we will show outsiders that we have the intestinal fortitude to combat the economic backslide that is taking place and 4) people of color can, at last, begin to get recognition for our many contributions to the life-chances of this city.

Third, and most profoundly, the City of Omaha needs to overturn its image of being a town full of hillbillies. Face it, every joke cracked about this city has something to do with our either being backwards, neanderthal or non-productive. None of these labels is the kind of fact or foundation on which to build a program that would bring business here. Therefore, negation of the actual and pursuance of the possible should be a project of paramount importance.

Negating the actual means we have to stop relying on outside information telling us what's wrong or how we can cure our ills. Omaha's small-town atmosphere and segregated social state both give a unique flavor to its needs and wants. Omahans know the people and area better than any New Yorker or Californian ever could. Omaha has qualified scholars in this city who could use consultant support, and finally, we merely inflame the belief that Omahans are dumb when we have to go elsewhere for advice, security and solace.
*

Pursuance of the possible means that those unavailed of sources of creativity and energy should be called upon. Because of the oftentimes discriminatory nature of the society we live in, people of color have been the true survivalists. Our economic and social state has always been one of living on a little.

Therefore, it seems that since the city is now in a similar state, the consultants should be those who have "felt the sting of the lash" or who have an understanding of this systems and how to survive in it. That would mean this area's most neglected residents: blacks, Chicanos, Native Americans and Asians.

A citywide program of "cultural inclusion" in areas outside of the artistic would be a step in the right direction.

At a time when people of color need jobs and the city administration is in obvious need of new and profound suggestions for fiscal control, it seems that a symbiotic relationship could finally develop. People of color certainly have skills in the area of surviving on a limited budget, and the city's budget is, to put it mildly, limited.

On the other hand, the city would do well to create programs and paradigms that provide "minorities" with the chance, channels and challenge of applying the many creative skills that we have at our disposal – skills that go beyond entertainment and athletics, I might add.

Omaha could learn a lesson from the "black power" advocates of the '60s. Carmichael and Hamilton (1972) wrote that, "before a group can enter open society, they must first close ranks." Before Omaha can be the model for the rest of the country, it must do the same thing and make use of what it has internally. And this means calling on Omahans regardless of race in dealing with a problem that is facing us all: the collapse of the economic system as we know it.

The key to a revitalized economy, provision of more jobs, a renewed self-esteem among all Omahans and actualization of the good life for all of us lies in promoting a united effort. For surely, the turning of that key will call for the collective resources of us all.

CONCLUSION

> In the twilight of materialism, the meaning of housing will be simplified and clarified, with a renewed emphasis on shelter and neighborhood. The false hope that everyone can get rich from real estate will be laid to rest for another fifty years, or perhaps for all time.
> **—John S. Adams, "Housing Markets in the Twilight of Materialism"**

Emerson once wrote that, "an institution is the length and shadow of a man." We cannot expect Anglo institutions to be all inclusive despite their grandiose claims that they are. In order to build institutions we must have components to use to develop to the institutional level. We can begin with courses and curricula that reflect and reinforce our views and values. This proposed Africentric Sociourban Planning paradigm has been one such contribution.

This book has been an introduction to what I call Africentric Sociourban Planning. It is a paradigm or model that addresses the demographic transition that this society is undergoing. No matter how the white man attempts to stall or circumvent reality, the fact is that his white nation – which became that way because of his genocidal warfare against First Nation people – is now becoming increasingly "brown." And by "brown" I mean "not white." And the majority of them cannot stand it, which is how President Donald Trump rose to power and why these white people are continually attempting to pawn themselves off as "victims." Malcolm X once referred to racism as "the hate that hate produced." He also said that the assassination of President Kennedy was a case of "the chickens coming home to roost."

Today, in 2018, a new paradigm is needed because the cities remain predominantly black and brown. The white man spewing out the orders and directions will no longer suffice. From now on, only results – led and determined by us – will suffice.

REFERENCES

Beauregard, Robert (2007). More than sector theory: Homer Hoyt's contributions to planning knowledge. **Journal of Planning History**, 6, (3).

Benjamin, R. (2012, March 29). "The gated community mentality," **New York Times.**

Davidson, Michael & Dolnick, Fay (Eds.) (2004). **A Planner's Dictionary**. Washington, D.C.: APA Planning Advisory Services.

Du Bois, W.E.B. (2003). **The Souls of black folk**. New York, New York: Barnes and Nobles Classics.

Erikson, a. (2012, August 24). A brief history of the birth of urban planning. **The Atlantic Cities.**

Hill, A.F. (2011). **Reimagining equality: Stories of gender, race, and finding home** (Boston, Massachusetts: Beacon Publishing.

Hill, A. F.(1995). "Marriage and patronage in the empowerment and disempowerment of African-American women," in **Race, Gender, and Power in America: The Legacy of the Hill-Thomas Hearings,** ed. Anita F. Hill and Emma Coleman Jordan (New York, New York: Oxford University Press.

Levy, John M. (2000). **Contemporary Urban Planning**. Upper Saddle River, New Jersey: Prentice-Hall.

Manning, June Thomas & Ritzdorf, Marsha (1997) **Urban Planning in the African American Community In the Shadows.** Belmont, California: Sage Publications. Retrieved from https://www.amazon.com/Urban-Planning-African-American-Community-Shadows/dp/0803972342

Massey, Douglas S. & Denton, Nancy A. (1993). **American Apartheid: Segregation and the Making of the Underclass.** Cambridge, Massachusetts: Harvard University Press.

Metzger, John T. (1996) The theory and practice of equity planning: An annotated bibliography. **Journal of Planning Literature**,11, (1).

National Public Radio. (2011, May 18). When The Levee Breaks: Ripples Of The Great Flood. All Things Considered. Retrieved from https://www.npr.org/2011/05/18/136427246/when-the-levee-breaks-ripples-of-the-great-flood

Newkirk, Vann R. II. (2018, February 28). Trump's EPA Concludes Environmental Racism is Real. **The Atlantic.** Retrieved from https://www.theatlantic.com/politics/archive/2018/02/the-trump-administration-finds-that-environmental-racism-is-real/554315/

Rugh, J.S. & Massey, D.S. (2010). "Racial segregation and the American foreclosure crisis," **American Sociological Review** 75, (5). 629-51.

Rury, John L. and Jeffrey E. Mirel. (1997). "The Political Economy of Urban Education." **Review of Research in Education,** 22.

Semuels, Alana (2016, March 18). The role of highways in American poverty. **The Atlantic.** Retrieved from https://www.theatlantic.com/business/archive/2016/03/role-of-highways-in-american-poverty/474282/

Taylor, Nigel (1998). **Urban Planning Theory Since 1945**. Los Angeles, California: Sage Publications.

White, Jeremy (2011, August 31). Minorities Are Majority in 22 Big Urban Areas, as America Reaches 'Demographic Tipping Point': Report. **International Business Times.** Retrieved from https://www.ibtimes.com/minorities-are-majority-22-big-urban-areas-america-reaches-demographic-tipping-point-report-307390

Wikipedia (2012). Wilmington insurrection of 1898. Retrieved from en.wikipedia.org/wiki/Wilmington_Insurrection_of_1898.

Wyly, Elvyn. Ponder, C.S., Nettling, Pierson, Ho, Bisco, Fung, Sophie Ellen, Liebowitz, Zachary and Hammel. (2012, September). New racial meanings of housing in America. *American Quarterly*, 64, 3.